T0291324

EXTRACURRICULAR ENTERPRISE AND ENTREPRENEURSHIP ACTIVITY

CONTEMPORARY ISSUES IN ENTREPRENEURSHIP RESEARCH

Series Editor, Volumes 1–6: Gerard McElwee
Volume 7 onward: Paul Jones

CONTEMPORARY ISSUES IN ENTREPRENEURSHIP
RESEARCH   VOLUME 19

EXTRACURRICULAR ENTERPRISE AND ENTREPRENEURSHIP ACTIVITY: A GLOBAL AND HOLISTIC PERSPECTIVE

EDITED BY

SARAH PREEDY

University of Plymouth, UK

AND

EMILY BEAUMONT

University of Gloucestershire, UK

United Kingdom – North America – Japan
India – Malaysia – China

Emerald Publishing Limited
Emerald Publishing, Floor 5, Northspring, 21-23 Wellington Street, Leeds LS1 4DL.

First edition 2024

Editorial matter and selection © 2024 Sarah Preedy and Emily Beaumont.
Individual chapters © 2024 The authors.
Published under exclusive licence by Emerald Publishing Limited.

Reprints and permissions service
Contact: www.copyright.com

No part of this book may be reproduced, stored in a retrieval system, transmitted in
any form or by any means electronic, mechanical, photocopying, recording or otherwise
without either the prior written permission of the publisher or a licence permitting
restricted copying issued in the UK by The Copyright Licensing Agency and in the USA
by The Copyright Clearance Center. Any opinions expressed in the chapters are those
of the authors. Whilst Emerald makes every effort to ensure the quality and accuracy of
its content, Emerald makes no representation implied or otherwise, as to the chapters'
suitability and application and disclaims any warranties, express or implied, to their use.

British Library Cataloguing in Publication Data
A catalogue record for this book is available from the British Library

ISBN: 978-1-80382-372-0 (Print)
ISBN: 978-1-80382-371-3 (Online)
ISBN: 978-1-80382-373-7 (Epub)

ISSN: 2040-7246 (Series)

Printed and bound by CPI Group (UK) Ltd, Croydon, CR0 4YY

INVESTOR IN PEOPLE

CONTENTS

LIST OF FIGURES AND TABLES

FIGURES

TABLES

ABOUT THE EDITORS

Dr Sarah Preedy is a Lecturer in Enterprise at the University of Plymouth. She teaches in the areas of Enterprise, Entrepreneurship, Innovation and Creativity. Her research focusses on the role, value and impact of Enterprise and Entrepreneurship education; most recently she has explored entrepreneurial learning through engagement in extracurricular enterprise activities and the development of entrepreneurial identity and intention in higher education students. She is a Senior Fellow of the Higher Education Academy, Fellow of Enterprise Educators UK and a Certified Management and Business Educator for the Chartered Association of Business Schools.

Dr Emily Beaumont is an Associate Professor of Enterprise and Entrepreneurship who has dedicated her teaching, research and practice to enterprise and entrepreneurship education. Emily is a former President and current Director of Enterprise Educators UK (EEUK), a membership organisation that enables excellence in enterprise and entrepreneurship education by connecting and supporting enterprise and entrepreneurship educators across the UK. Emily is also an Active Member of the AGCAS (Association of Graduate Careers and Advisory Services) Enterprise and Entrepreneurship Task Group, Director of ISBE (Institute for Small Business and Entrepreneurship) and Co-Chair of the Research in Enterprise and Entrepreneurship Education Special Interest Group, a collaboration between EEUK and ISBE.

ABOUT THE CONTRIBUTORS

Paul Benedict, Ohio University, USA, is a Seed-stage Investor, Executive and Entrepreneur bringing 14 years of industry experience to the classroom. Paul teaches entrepreneurship in the Professional MBA Program and Management in the Integrated Business Cluster. Paul earned his BA in Political Science from the Honours Tutorial College at Ohio University. He earned his MBA from the Fisher College of Business at The Ohio State University.

Eleanor Browne, Coventry University, UK, is the Managing Director of Coventry University Social Enterprise CIC, providing extracurricular entrepreneurship training and startup support for the group's students, graduates and staff. Before this, she spent four years at The University of Queensland, Australia, supporting and enabling the embedding of entrepreneurial education in the curriculum across all disciplines. She began her university incubation career at the University of Plymouth, UK, where for 10 years she led the business incubation services.

Eleanor's PhD is in Business Incubation and her broader research interests are at the intersection of entrepreneurial education, collaboration and learning. She is a Certified Innovation Practitioner and Associate Fellow of the Higher Education Academy.

Katarina Ellborg is Senior Lecturer at the School of Business and Economics at Linnaeus University, Sweden. In her work, she has adopted *Didaktik* on entrepreneurship education in higher education with a student-centred approach. She has, for example, developed and examined a visual-based teaching exercise in order to explore students' understandings of entrepreneurship. Her interest in visual methods and interpretative research traditions has also led to explorations of educational tools in general, and illustrations of business models in particular. Current research also includes entrepreneurship in the cultural field, in which she combines her interests in art and entrepreneurship.

Krystal Geyer, Ohio University, USA, Associate Director and Assistant Professor of Instruction. Strong higher education professional skilled in entrepreneurship, academic advising, student involvement, teaching and program management. Entrepreneurship educator, devoted student affairs professional, educating others through passion, excitement and fun. Constantly striving to make a difference.

Felicity Healey-Benson, is Lead Researcher and Entrepreneurial Learning Champion within the International Institute for Creative Entrepreneurial Development at UWTSD. She is a Serial Academic Entrepreneur, founding several successful ventures, including 'Emergent Thinkers.com', Harmonious

Entrepreneurship Society (Harmonious Entrepreneurship Ltd.) with Professor David A. Kirby, and a phenomenological learned society, 'hanfod.NL' in collaboration with Dr. Mike Johnson. These ventures are dedicated to identifying and disseminating new educational, research and business practices that promote sustainability and support wider economic and social development. As an EntreComp Champion she is committed to advancing teachers' entrepreneurial education skills globally through online CPD opportunities, underpinned by the European Entrepreneurship Competence Framework. Additionally, she has co-developed an innovative online Postgraduate Certificate in Education Skills. She is also credited as the Originator of the 'Professional Context Vlog' and among other publications has contributed to and supported the editing of 'Applying Sustainability: Principles and Practices', authored by Tay, Kay Luan, in 2019.

Paul J. Jackson, is a Principal Lecturer in the Oxford Brookes Business School, where he teaches and researches in the area of Information Systems and Digital Entrepreneurship. In recent times, he has also headed the University's experiential learning initiative, the Business Challenge Week – liaising with academic colleagues and external clients to recruit and coordinate student teams and external partners. Paul also has a background in Executive Education and Management Consultancy, and has acted as an Oxford Brookes Liaison Manager for several collaborative international programmes, including its biggest franchise arrangement, with the Chengdu University of Technology.

David A. Kirby, was Founding Dean and Vice President of the British University in Egypt, from 2007 to 2017, in which capacity he introduced entrepreneurship education to the University and the country. Prior to this, he had pioneered the teaching of entrepreneurship in the UK and internationally, and held one of the UK's first Entrepreneurship chairs at Durham University Business School, from 1988 to 1996. At Surrey University, he not only introduced innovative new undergraduate and postgraduate programmes but, in 2003, the first SETsquared incubator on the Surrey University Research Park. He holds Honorary Professorships at Almaty Management University in Kazakhstan and the University of Wales Trinity St. David and is the Co-founder (with Dr. Felicity Healey-Benson) of the Harmonious Entrepreneurship Society (https://harmonious-entrepreneurship. org). He has published 160 journal articles and 18 books and research monographs, including "Entrepreneurship" (McGraw-Hill, 2003). He holds various international awards for his contribution to entrepreneurship and, in 2006, was a lifetime recipient of The Queen's Award for Enterprise Promotion.

Jonathan Louw, is Principal Lecturer (teaching, learning and student experience) based in the Oxford Brookes Business School. He is also the School lead in relation to the United Nations Principles for the Responsible Management Education initiative. His undergraduate teaching is focused on sustainability and employability, with postgraduate teaching centred on the CIPD accredited Masters in HRM programmes. His other roles include Liaison Manager for the Dual Degree (European Business) offered with the University of Applied Sciences,

Regensburg, Germany. He is also a Mentor on the HEA Professional Standards Framework pathway run by the Oxford Centre for Academic Enhancement and Development.

Andrea Macrae, is Principal Lecturer in Education, Student Experience and Stylistics in the School of Humanities, Education and Languages at Oxford Brookes University, and is the Faculty Employability and Enterprise Education Lead. She teaches, researches and publishes in the areas of stylistics, narratology, world literature and cognitive poetics. Most recently, she has been developing modules that bring together literature and sustainability, and English studies and entrepreneurship. She is also interested in student skills literacy, employability and enterprise within HE English, and has run several large-scale projects on these issues.

Nicolette Michels is Associate Dean in the Oxford Brookes Business School, where she has responsibility for leading programme innovation and renewal across the School's undergraduate, postgraduate and professional education portfolio. She was the University lead on the award of Small Business Charter and previously AMBA accreditations. She has taught on Bachelors, Masters and MBA programmes, including modules in Enterprise, Consultancy, Marketing and Leadership. She currently leads developments in live student projects and embedding of in-curricular enterprise.

Nicolai Nybye, the Department of Applied Research in Business and Technology, UCL University College, Denmark, is researching the meaning-making in entrepreneurial processes as these unfold in contexts of both business and non-business education. In this, he investigates more paradoxical evidence of entrepreneurship in curricular education and as extracurricular activities. His research challenges one-size-fits all tendencies in entrepreneurship education to address possibilities and barriers for students to engage with meaning in innovation and entrepreneurship courses and projects. He has wide professional experience from practice in companies, own firm, voluntary work and the academic field as educator and researcher.

Luke Pittaway, Ohio University, USA, is the Copeland Professor of Entrepreneurship at Ohio University and a Justin G. Longenecker Fellow at USASBE. His research focuses on entrepreneurship education and learning. He has a range of other interests including: entrepreneurial behaviour, networking, entrepreneurial failure, business growth and corporate venturing. In 2018, he was nominated and selected to be USASBE's Entrepreneurship Educator of the Year.

Michael Breum Ramsgaard, is an Associate Professor at VIA University College, Aarhus, Denmark. He is affiliated with the Research Centre for Innovation & Entrepreneurship. He has 15 years of research experience in the area of entrepreneurship education, entrepreneurial learning and innovation management. In 2015, he was awarded a prize for his work from Danish Society for Entrepreneurship and Business. His research interests are all within entrepreneurship education, with a special focus on experiential learning, teaching and pedagogical development and context. His research has been published in Innovations in Education and Teaching International and Education + Training.

Tatiana Somià, Ohio University, USA, Researcher, Consultant, Educator. Skilled in Human Resource Management and Entrepreneurial Competency Development. Focused on entrepreneurial and female competencies, education and learning. Specialties include management development and training, professional training, coaching university students, organisational development, evaluation processes and competency analysis.

Lucy Turner, is Interim Associate Dean for Education and Student Experience in the Faculty of Technology, Design and Environment at Oxford Brookes. She works with programme teams to enhance their delivery and helps them embed university strategy into their programmes in order to improve the quality of teaching and learning. She is focused on the enhancement of the student experience and the significance of student partnerships within the development of an inclusive curriculum. She is also the School of Arts' Enterprise and Employability Lead, working on employability projects and connecting with industry, thereby supporting students to grow their confidence in their career journeys.

Birgitte Wraae, is a researcher at the Chair of Entrepreneurship and Innovation Management at Technische Universität Berlin, Germany. Her research interests are in entrepreneurship, especially entrepreneurship education: the role of the entrepreneurship educator, identity formation, emancipation and reflection. She excels in doing research in connection with the entrepreneurial learning space. Her research has been published in a range of journals. She is a skilled educator and has been teaching and supervising entrepreneurship for more than 10 years. Currently, she is embedding entrepreneurship and entrepreneurial learning approaches into other topics. She has authored a book about the entrepreneurial learning journey and how the entrepreneurship educator can facilitate that journey.

PREFACE

At any level of education, extracurricular activities have often been seen as a bolt-on to what is happening within the classroom. Ad hoc, lacking theoretical grounding, a value added extra, extracurricular activities have been viewed as a poor relation of the core curriculum. However, in higher education (HE), this view is increasingly outdated as industry and society calls for, and students respond to, the need for experiences beyond their degree. HE students wanting to showcase a collection of skills, behaviours and competencies recognise that evidence of these can be achieved outside of the classroom in the realms of the extracurricular. Consequently, the scope of extracurricular activities is growing and morphing with changing demand and the socio-economic climate.

Extracurricular activities are a key element of any university's entrepreneurial ecosystem with numerous studies emphasising the need for a holistic approach whereby extracurricular and in-curricular activities compliment and connect each other (Harima, Gießelmann, Göttsch, & Schlichting, 2021; Preedy & Jones, 2015, 2017). Yet, in practice, this synergy has not been easy to achieve. Early studies examining extracurricular enterprise activities, such as Rae, Martin, Antcliff, and Hannon (2012), noted the diversity of extracurricular enterprise and entrepreneurship activities available to students but also recognised its precarity as external funding came to an end, or management switched hands and/or changed tack. However, now universities are increasingly assured of the value of enterprise and entrepreneurship education both in and out of the curriculum, they are beginning to provide and support a sustainable extracurricular offer (Preedy, Jones, Maas, & Duckett, 2020).

In response to the increasing interest and demand for extracurricular activities, and to support their growth and sustainability of provision we have created this book to serve all those who are engaged or have an interest in enterprise and entrepreneurship extracurricular education. To that end, we have considered a range of perspectives. Contributions are made from across the world, giving a global context that considers the diversity in enterprise and entrepreneurship extracurricular activities appeal and role, resourcing and challenges, alongside innovative and impactful practice in design and delivery. Additionally, and in keeping with Enterprise Educators UK's presentation of the enterprise and entrepreneurship educator, we write for the Academic, Practitioner, and Influencer identities, with each chapter containing academic discussion, suggestions for improving teaching and learning/practitioner practice, and recommendations for policy.

The result is a book which contributes important insights, evaluations and evidence of the role and value of extracurricular enterprise and entrepreneurship activities. However, it also recognises that there is still further work to be done to understand and capture the ongoing and evolving value and impact of these activities. Subsequently through this book we hope to shine a light on an under-represented area of enterprise and entrepreneurship education to encourage discussion and development of practice and policy but also to fuel the appreciation, understanding and impact of this topic.

REFERENCES

Harima, A., Gießelmann, J., Göttsch, V., & Schlichting, L. (2021). Entrepreneurship? Let us do it later: Procrastination in the intention–behavior gap of student entrepreneurship. *International Journal of Entrepreneurial Behavior & Research, 27*(5), 1189–1213.

Preedy, S., & Jones, P. (2015). An investigation into University extra-curricular enterprise support provision. *Education + Training, 57*(8/9), 992–1008.

Preedy, S., & Jones, P. (2017). Student-led enterprise groups and entrepreneurial learning: A UK perspective. *Industry and Higher Education, 31*(2), 101–112.

Preedy, S., Jones, P., Maas, G., & Duckett, H. (2020). Examining the perceived value of extracurricular enterprise activities in relation to entrepreneurial learning processes. *Journal of Small Business and Enterprise Development, 27*(7), 1085–1105.

Rae, D., Martin, L., Antcliff, V., & Hannon, P. (2012). Enterprise and entrepreneurship in English higher education: 2010 and beyond. *Journal of Small Business and Enterprise Development, 19*(3), 380–401.

ACKNOWLEDGEMENTS

The editors would like to thank the dynamic and inspirational community of enterprise and entrepreneurship educators, researchers and practitioners we work with on a daily basis. Without the advances in knowledge resulting from the work of such groups, a book like this would not be possible. We hope this book supports you all in your enterprise and entrepreneurship journey.

CHAPTER 1

ENTREPRENEURSHIP CLUBS AND SOCIETIES: LEARNING BENEFITS IN PRACTICE

Luke Pittaway, Paul Benedict, Krystal Geyer and Tatiana Somià

Department of Management, Ohio University, Athens, OH, USA

ABSTRACT

This chapter provides an overview of entrepreneurship clubs. It charts the development of these organisations, as a form of extracurricular activity. It introduces different forms of entrepreneurship clubs, such as Junior Achievement (JA) and Enactus, and explains how they grew from 1919 to the present. It also illustrates the differences between self-organised clubs, organised programs using clubs as a learning method, structured societies and nationally organised cooperative societies. The second part introduces research on student clubs in entrepreneurship education. It explores the benefits of clubs. It shows that clubs assist student learning, enable the acquisition of practical skills and improve college attendance, employment opportunities and career attainment. We argue that entrepreneurship clubs have improved student learning outcomes in entrepreneurship and simulated entrepreneurial learning, while impacting student self-efficacy and intentionality as well as improving employability and social learning. The final part of the chapter provides advice and tips for educators advising student-run entrepreneurship clubs. Ultimately, the chapter

Extracurricular Enterprise and Entrepreneurship Activity: A Global and Holistic Perspective
Contemporary Issues in Entrepreneurship Research, Volume 19, 1–14
Copyright © 2024 by Luke Pittaway, Paul Benedict, Krystal Geyer and Tatiana Somià
Published under exclusive licence by Emerald Publishing Limited
ISSN: 2040-7246/doi:10.1108/S2040-724620240000019001

explains how student clubs have developed, why they are important for student learning and how advisors can support them.

Keywords: Clubs; societies; extracurriculars; entrepreneurship; experiential learning; entrepreneurial learning

INTRODUCTION

Imagine walking into a bar and seeing a group of young people huddled together, debating and drinking. You can hear them talking about the latest technologies and potential ventures they could create. It turns out the group is meeting as part of an organised club. The next day, you visit the local coffee house where another club is meeting. They are supping coffee and arguing about how best to help their community through a social venture. Clubs and societies have a long history and have contributed to the development of democracies and institutions while becoming increasingly focused on niche topics and interests, including entrepreneurship, as demonstrated in the previous example. Pittaway, Rodriguez-Falcon, Aiyegbayo, and King (2011, p. 39) defined such entrepreneurship clubs as,

> informal, non-accredited student-led societies or clubs whose main goal is to attract students who are interested in learning about enterprise and developing enterprising skills to either start their own businesses or to become more enterprising people.

These informal, loose arrangements of like-minded people have led to impactful change in society. Today, the extracurricular entrepreneurship club has become particularly vibrant and grown across countries, offering a way for young people to lead entrepreneurial change.

The authors aim to chart the growth and development of extracurricular entrepreneurship clubs and will provide a historical overview of the development of these extracurricular activities. They introduce the key types of clubs in entrepreneurship education. Their goal is to explain the educational drive underlying the founding of these activities. The authors will explain what benefits accrue to students from engagement in clubs and draw on prior research on the subject. They introduce what is known about their value, describe the benefits for students and explain why students engage with them. They expand on the knowledge of extracurricular activity in entrepreneurship education by examining the value of entrepreneurship clubs. Finally, they consider best practices for advising entrepreneurship extracurricular activities.

METHODOLOGY

The authors throughout have drawn on previous literature in discussing the history of extracurricular entrepreneurship education in the USA and the UK. These are the two areas of focus because of their rich history in the subject matter and their importance in the early founding of entrepreneurship and other special interest clubs, societies and organisations. As the chapter advances towards offering advice and best practices, the authors draw on experience and observational data to provide advice to educators and give useful, actionable guidance.

EXTRACURRICULAR ENTREPRENEURSHIP EDUCATION – THE HISTORY OF DIFFERENT TYPES

During the 17th and 18th centuries, clubs and societies became an important aspect in the fabric of civil society in Britain and its overseas territories (Clark, 2000). These 'self-organising groups' spread across a wide range of interests, including sports, education, politics, religion, music and philanthropy, providing the foundation for many institutions that grew out of largely informal associations (e.g. chambers of commerce, freemasons, trade associations, etc.). Clark (2000) links this rapid increase in volunteerism to urbanisation, the rising availability of social time and the opening of religious independence and secularism. The first student clubs were founded at Oxford and Cambridge universities (1729). Many luminaries of the period belonged to clubs; for example, Adam Smith was a member of Edinburgh's Literary Club and John Adams was a member of Boston's Hunting Club. Many clubs had learning and educational aims or were focused on aspects of venturing and are the forbearers of today's entrepreneurship clubs. These clubs were both social and professional and often met in pubs and coffeehouses. As they grew, many became institutionalised and took on their own spaces (Clark, 2000).

The first extracurricular entrepreneurship education can be linked to the founding of JA in the USA in 1919. It was offered to high school students as an after-school club engaging students in the establishment of ventures. The British version of JA, Young Enterprise (YE), was founded in 1962, while the European version (JADE – European Confederation of Junior Enterprises) started in 1967 focused on university students. JADE, in contrast to JA and YE, involved the establishment of non-profit organisations, engaged students in consulting projects and provided them with experience running a company (Almeida, Daniel, & Figueiredo, 2021). In all three cases, the organisations were created by external stakeholders who wished to provide young people with 'business skills', and were not 'self-organising', as is implied in the definition of a club or society.

Entrepreneurship clubs, therefore, precede the development of modern entrepreneurship education. Today's forms of entrepreneurship clubs have expanded with the growth of formal education in entrepreneurship. The first in this wave was Students in Free Enterprise (SIFE), now Enactus, founded in 1975 by the National Leadership Institute. Its original aim was to get students more interested in free enterprise. As it grew, it gained significant corporate sponsorship and morphed to focus on social enterprise and community volunteering, taking an entrepreneurial approach to solving local problems. Enactus students formed university chapters, engaged in social enterprise projects and competed in regional and national competitions.

In 1983, the Association of Collegiate Entrepreneurs (later Collegiate Entrepreneurs' Organisation or CEO) was started as a conference supporting student entrepreneurs in the Midwest US. Gerry Hills, a Professor at the University of Illinois Chicago, facilitated the first meeting along with John Hughes and Jean Thorne of the Coleman Foundation. CEO was designed to support individual student entrepreneurs and university-based clubs. Though data are scarce, self-organised entrepreneurship clubs probably existed in US universities prior to the establishment of CEO. Like its modern Finnish counterparts, the CEO was established with significant social considerations, providing a space for students to interact and meet, alongside its professional aims to promote entrepreneurship clubs.

As the 1990s and 2000s saw growth and expansion of entrepreneurship education, US style clubs expanded internationally. Students at UK universities began self-organised entrepreneurship clubs. They formed the Association of Student Entrepreneurs (ASE), gained UK government funding, and became the National Association of College and University Entrepreneurs (NACUE) (Preedy & Jones, 2017). In 1995, Enactus grew internationally, entering the UK in 2002. Other countries, notably Finland, joined the trend and have seen growth in their student-led entrepreneurship societies (Parkkari & Kohtakangas, 2018; Siivonen, Peura, Hytti, Kasanen, & Komulainen, 2020). Other forms of individual entrepreneurship clubs have proliferated. In addition to the types mentioned, there are also entrepreneurship fraternities (e.g. Epsilon Nu Tau and Sigma Eta Pi), maker societies, design, consulting, social entrepreneurship, seed-capital finance clubs, etc. These are usually self-organised by students but are sometimes sponsored by entrepreneurship centres.

This history illustrates that there are several forms of organisational approach at work within extracurricular entrepreneurship education. A useful distinction can be made between clubs, which are self-governing, and societies that are more institutionalised with clearer rules and procedures, although both sit alongside national organisations designed to coordinate activities and share best practices (Brew, 1943). A similar distinction is made in entrepreneurship where several forms are identified (Pittaway et al., 2011; Pittaway, Gazzard, Shore, & Williamson, 2015).

Since the 1980s, entrepreneurship clubs and societies have grown in importance within entrepreneurship education and this momentum continues to gather pace. Entrepreneurship clubs have a long history, which predates the beginning of modern forms of entrepreneurship education. Students, advisors and others consider them to be important for student learning and the empirical research on the subject has gained momentum (Rubin, Bommer, & Baldwin, 2002). Next, the authors consider why these learning opportunities are attractive to young people and what benefits they bring.

LEARNING BENEFITS OF ENTREPRENEURSHIP CLUBS AND SOCIETIES

Early educational researchers were concerned that extracurricular entrepreneurship education might subvert formal educational activities, and this concern continues (Terenzini, Pascarella, & Blimling, 1999). Research has, however, increasingly demonstrated the value of student self-governing clubs for student learning (Rubin et al., 2002). Studies have illustrated the value of club involvement for the development of practical skills (Burggraaf, 1997), noted their importance to recruiters (Rutter & Jones, 2007), and highlighted their impact on college attendance (Mahoney, Cairns, & Farmer, 2003) and career attainment (Boone, Kurtz, & Fleenor, 1988).

Looking at learning, research has shown that involvement enhances interpersonal skills (Burggraaf, 1997), improves opportunities for practical application (Evans & Evans, 2001) and widens engagement with communities of practice (Block & French, 1991). Research has linked clubs with improved learning from mistakes (Grinder, Cooper, & Britt, 1999); the development of stronger oral, written, management and enterprise skills (Montes & Collazo, 2003); and enhanced motivation and self-confidence (McCorkle, Alexander, Reardon, & Kling, 2003). Though many prior studies were based on anecdote and experience, rather than empirical research, more comprehensive studies have confirmed this picture (Rubin et al., 2002). There are also noteworthy benefits accruing to founders and leaders of clubs, that likely encourage ambitious students to take the initiative to start new clubs, as well as take on executive leadership roles in established ones (Pittaway et al., 2015).

Faced with the growth in provision and interest in entrepreneurship clubs, researchers have begun to explore the benefits (Preedy & Jones, 2017). Clubs gain support from universities, national organisations, individual donors, corporate sponsors and national governments, with the confirmation that they provide value. Studies have begun to unpick tangible benefits of extracurricular entrepreneurship education for students. Pittaway et al. (2011), for example, show a range of learning outcomes including students learning by doing, increased reflective learning and value from social learning. They also observed transformative learning from critical moments accrued from mistakes and failures experienced. They also noted that certain aspects of entrepreneurial learning, such as experiencing uncertainty, ambiguity and emotional exposure were observed less often.

Taking the topic further, Pittaway et al. (2015) expanded the prior qualitative study and conducted a survey of students. They found that 'accommodating learning' stood out as a major benefit. This type of learning implied students were engaged in active experimentation and gained experience from managing clubs and leading projects. Such experience was also contextual and situated, so that it was relevant to specific forms of entrepreneurial effort engaged in (Pittaway et al., 2015). 'Assimilating learning' was also highlighted. Students got close to the 'lived experience' of entrepreneurs, through speakers and consulting projects, and this led them to greater insights and learning socially from their 'community of practice'.

Recent studies have built on this work. Almeida et al. (2021) studied Junior Enterprises (JE) and showed that JE members gain practical experience, get opportunities to network with business professionals, develop entrepreneurial and management skills, and improve their employability, leading to an entrepreneurial 'spirit'. They demonstrate that JE students have higher perceived behavioural control and have an improved perception that they can act as an entrepreneur. They also confirm a link between engagement in clubs and improved entrepreneurial intent (Almeida et al., 2021). Students are considered more likely to engage in entrepreneurial activity after being involved in a JE company. Arranz, Ubierna, Arroyabe, Perez, and Fdez. de Arroyabe (2017) and Padilla-Angulo (2019) observe the same relationship, linking club involvement to increased entrepreneurial self-efficacy and intent.

Preedy and Jones (2017) highlight the continued growth of clubs in UK entrepreneurship education; with NACUE growing from 30-member organisations in 2011 to 64 by 2013. Their research confirms the role of experimentation, learning by doing and illustrates a general frustration, among participating students, with traditional higher education curricula. They also confirm the importance of clubs for improving interpersonal, communication, people and enterprise skills, as highlighted elsewhere (Burggraaf, 1997; Montes & Collazo, 2003). Like other studies, they find a surprising connection to motivations and benefits aimed at improved 'employability', alongside narrower aims focused on leading entrepreneurial endeavours. The importance of social learning is confirmed; groups link closely with their communities of practice via networking to gain access to knowledge, mentoring and finance. In this study, the benefits are higher for leaders of clubs and projects (Pittaway et al., 2015).

The research on the learning benefits of entrepreneurship clubs highlights consensus around why students engage with them and why they are helpful for student learning. Entrepreneurship clubs vary, adopting aspects of local culture and cross a spectrum from loose arrangements to corporate-sponsored international organisations. These are self-organising groups of young people, who want to have fun and meet each other. Alongside this social function, clubs have professional aims to support enterprise skills, venture creation and aim to improve employability (Brew, 1943). There are many learning benefits; students learn by doing, become more reflective practitioners, social learning allows them to gain from peers and grow closer to their target communities of practice. They pick up interpersonal, communication, people and enterprise skills to assist them as a founder or employee clubs improve self-efficacy and intentionality for taking on entrepreneurial efforts and thus help encourage students to take the plunge.

Given these benefits, universities, centres for entrepreneurship, employers, governments and corporate sponsors are keen to use extracurricular activities to support entrepreneurship education. As these are 'self-organising groups of young people', there are many challenges in managing clubs and these considerations are next.

ADVISING ENTREPRENEURSHIP CLUBS AND SOCIETIES

As extracurricular entrepreneurship education opportunities are led by students and combine social and professional aims, advising them brings challenges. The role of the advisor is fraught with tensions; advisors want clubs to be successful, but students should take the lead, learn through their experience and be allowed to fail. Advisors also have ethical and legal responsibilities. They are expected to prevent hazing and must monitor behaviour while ensuring students properly represent their institution. Advisors are called upon to make sure students follow relevant codes of conduct, both internal to the institution and maintaining adherence to any local or federal laws, and operate their activities or organisations ethically. Meanwhile, students want space away from their formal academic experience, often prefer minimal direction and engage in socialising, which can be problematic. Due to these tensions, it can be difficult to balance between overzealous micromanaging and an anything goes, *laissez-faire* approach. We consider some of the common issues faced and make suggestions for advisors.

Getting Started

Club startup processes offer some considerations. If educators or entrepreneurship centres wish to establish a new club, the startup process ought to be led by students and advisors might have to first demonstrate the benefit of the club. So how does one guide the effort to get a new club started when no students have expressed an interest? As students appreciate the employability benefits from starting or leading a club, faculty are sometimes invited to be advisors of new efforts, even when there appears to be little demand or the proposed club duplicates existing ones. Another question arises: How do you manage student expectations for new efforts and channel them productively? In both situations, entrepreneurship programs need to be proactive. It is important to have a strategic view about which and how clubs are to be supported, taking into consideration the number of clubs and membership. This requires thought and can impact how entrepreneurship programs are evaluated and ranked. As programs aim to promote student initiative, it is also important to be flexible and open to student proposals, to encourage learning by doing and not be too wedded to prior strategic decisions.

Advisors can still support the establishment of a club but need to recognise that the club's foundation must be student-led. A common technique is to headhunt a founding team, either via recommendations, cherry-picking known student leaders or assessments of academic performance seeking students in disciplines relevant to the new club or its executive roles. Student founders must be motivated. Just like startups, getting the right team at the beginning can make an outsized difference later. The advisor taking time to target key leaders and engage in 'selling the value' of founding a club is worth the effort. Recruiting to four roles at the outset (e.g. President, Vice-President, Recruitment Chair and Treasurer) is recommended. Other efforts by the advisor can help, such as finding stakeholders (e.g. advisory boards and company sponsors), who are willing to raise awareness and help the club.

Dealing With Bureaucracy

Though entrepreneurship clubs are self-organising, most universities have governance structures that must be followed. In the USA, these are led by campus involvement centres, student senates, and sorority and fraternity offices, while in

the UK, student unions provide this oversight. Institutions have varying expectations including bylaws, training, funding and recruitment support, compliance,
and assistance with financial accounts. Student leaders are expected to navigate
these requirements on behalf of the club. Advisors are wise to take a role. Being
aware of these expectations is a minimum obligation, but advisors are encouraged
to meet with representatives from the governing body. Club operation is often
impeded when student executives fail to complete their bureaucratic function
(e.g. registering as a student club, completing financial reports, engaging in
required training), and it is important that advisors are aware if clubs are about
to break compliance rules (e.g. serving alcohol at a function, posting fliers where
they are not allowed, etc.). Though we want students to learn by doing and fail
occasionally, the advisor needs to be on hand to help students navigate these
bureaucratic requirements.

Building Structures, Getting Organised and Recruiting

One of the first decisions a club needs to make concerns the foundational structure
of the organisation, deciding whether to adopt an in-house or franchise model
(e.g. self-organised or an affiliated chapter). This decision has many downstream
effects, both positive and negative. A club built in-house may require a longer
start-up period but allows substantially more freedom in building a business
model, influencing the planning and management of student-targeted resources,
while keeping students focused on campus-specific impact. Choosing a self-built
structure, however, can take a long time to implement.

A franchise model (e.g. Epsilon Nu Tau or Enactus) in contrast can assist a
quicker start-up via the adoption of an established business model, well-defined
structures and operating procedures, but does not allow for customised procedures, flexible schedules and total control of finances. Some franchise models
(e.g. professional fraternities) also take a cut of membership fees/fundraising which
can impact downstream viability. Other franchise models (e.g. Enactus) can offer
additional resources and opportunities that might not be available otherwise.
Carefully considering the purpose of the club and the best model is worthwhile.

Because clubs are largely structured around a shared interest, it is important to
avoid homogeny among club members. Diversity, equity and inclusion should be
a key components in a recruitment strategy, as this is an important way to avoid
groupthink and consider a variety of experiences and perspectives. One strategy
to increase the likelihood of diversity in clubs is to avoid restrictive barriers to
entry or involvement, like expensive membership fees or requiring members to be
in a specific program of study.

Students are the key resource of entrepreneurial clubs, recruitment strategy
and procedures are thus of strategic importance to birth, growth and long-term
success. Universities host many clubs that compete for new members and there
can be a bias towards starting new clubs. Establishing a recruitment strategy,
developing innovative procedures for attracting talented students, and publicis-
ing the club's mission and initiatives are consequently of importance. Advisors
ought to pay close attention to recruitment efforts led by students, to ensure club

executives use all the resources available to them for recruitment purposes and build a viable recruitment and retention strategy. Suggestions for a recruitment strategy include participating in involvement fairs, soliciting recommendations from current members or faculty, and visiting classes to spread information.

Managing Succession Planning

It is not unusual to experience situations where a dynamic and motivated team builds a club entrepreneurially, only for the club to decline rapidly once the transition to a new team occurs. Founders are often some of our most accomplished and entrepreneurial students and sometimes clubs can get off to a flying start. Poor succession planning though can leave the club without a strong team to build on the initial successes. This is a common experience, as students will regularly cycle through clubs as they get involved, grow into the role and then graduate.

Though there is a natural unavoidable flux and flow in the life of clubs, as teams come and go, it is valuable for advisors to ensure leadership teams are engaged in succession planning. The development and application of effective succession plans have been observed to help manage this ebb and flow. To aid in succession planning, standard operating procedures, peer training on responsibilities and strong bookkeeping are recommended.

Institutional Representation and Behaviour

An additional component to consider is that clubs frequently have an element of external relations. Programs send club members to competitions, organise guest speakers, facilitate meetings with donors and go on professional visits. Members can, and often do, represent the university with external stakeholders and partners. Clubs, however, can have a strong social component, which can sometimes involve drinking and other questionable behaviour. Advisors need to establish and maintain a strong code of conduct for students. In practice, this could mean reviewing the university's code of conduct regularly, asking students to submit questions for a guest speaker in advance, and setting expectations for activities. It is good practice to have a pre-departure or pre-event meeting with participants to remind them of their status as university representatives and help them to define what this means and what acceptable behaviour, dress, activities, etc., might look like. If the university is funding or sponsoring the event or trip, it can be helpful to have students sign an agreed contract of behaviour, holding them financially accountable for their portion of the costs if minimum standards are not met.

In the USA, and increasingly elsewhere, advisors must be aware of hazing rules and regulations relevant to their jurisdiction. Most universities have anti-hazing rules that can disqualify student clubs from operating on campus and increasingly US states have anti-hazing laws, such as the 2021 Colin's Law in Ohio (Section 2903.31 of the Ohio Revised Code). The law makes hazing a third-degree felony when it involves drugs or alcohol and holds advisors liable if they fail to act. Similar laws exist elsewhere, while important for preventing hazing, they also increase the risks for advisors if their approach is too *laissez-faire*. Advisors must be knowledgeable about policies and their liability.

Mentoring of Student Leaders

Taking on an advisor role implies becoming a mentor for members of the club and the executive team. Like all mentoring, these relationships come with important responsibilities. For advisors, it is important to help students navigate university bureaucracy, build sustainable organisations and ensure that leaders are prepared to handle the various challenges of their roles. For many students, this can be the first time they have taken on a leadership duty and, consequently, mentors have responsibilities to help students develop professionally (e.g. networking or communication skills, etc.). Mentoring relationships can depend on the compatibility of the two parties and sometimes it can be the responsibility of the advisor to find other mentors well-matched with a student leader, and not always take on these duties alone. Successful mentorship arrangements can help individual club leaders grow, indirectly impacting the club and its quality, by growing leadership competence.

Being a good mentor for club executives can be challenging, which can depend on individual relationships as well as the size and dynamism of the club. As clubs become established it thus becomes important to consider mentorship a team effort, where the use of a board of advisors and the engagement of alumni become vital. The advisor becomes more of a broker of relationships, sourcing effective mentors for leaders and monitoring of the relationships.

Productive mentoring relationships also require mentees to take on certain responsibilities, such as setting explicit goals and objectives for the relationship, and organising to meet the mentor on a regular basis. Given the implied good will of alumni, advisors must also check that student leaders are upholding their relationship responsibilities. Meeting with student leaders early on and collaboratively setting expectations from both parties can be helpful.

Performing to Expectations

When students represent the university externally at competitions and events, advisors need to make sure they are performing appropriately and representing their institution positively. In US competitions, placement and prize money won are considered in rankings and student club performance becomes doubly valuable for programs. Strong student performance leads to positive press and storytelling that can bolster recruitment, fundraising and reputation. Best practices to ensure strong performance include conducting pitch practices, offering to proofread application materials and generally making sure students feel supported before they attend.

Depending on the type of event or interaction, advisors can also arrange etiquette dinners, facilitate mock interviews and give presentations on how to conduct successful networking. To the extent that the university or organisation is able, it is valuable to arrange for student organisation members to have business cards and access to appropriate apparel.

Advisors should also be cautious about assuming students have prior knowledge of things that seem obvious or commonplace, such as the proper way to compose a business-appropriate email or how to conduct oneself at a formal business dinner. Each type of organisation (e.g. Enactus vs. CEO or NACUE) has different requirements and advisors need to ensure they understand these obligations so that they can advise students accordingly.

Motivation, Disengagement and Resilience

As clubs are recognised by recruiters to have value, it is not unusual for students to become members and leaders of a club without a genuine motivation to engage. Experience has also revealed students sometimes join too many clubs and do not engage thoroughly. Club poor performance, weak student leadership and unclear aims and objectives can lead students to disengage. It is also evident, following COVID-19, that lower student resilience has made it more difficult to encourage engagement in extracurricular activities generally.

Poor- or ill-conceived motivations, overcommitment and student disengagement are common factors that impact student club survival and success. Advisors have a role by being involved in the selection process of student executives by aiming to avoid recruitment of the resume-builders and overcommitted students. They also play a function, carefully supporting the student executives, so that they learn how to engage and retain student members. Advisors can provide recruitment support and resources to help sell the value of engagement for student professional development, entrepreneurial skills and employment. Avoiding disengagement is another reason it is critical for clubs to be student-led.

Alumni Development

Entrepreneurship clubs need support from within the institution and from outside. External support often includes alumni, corporate sponsors and members of the local community. A good alumni engagement strategy can provide invaluable benefits for the club by bringing free advice, resources and financial support.

University alumni relations offices are often willing to provide advisors with access to alumni who might have an affinity with the club's mission. Donor relations officers are often motivated to help secure resources for the club from such interested alumni. Advisors can highlight to students the diversity of the alumni body in terms of age, beliefs, location, background and other attributes. Different clubs will need to build an engagement strategy around the club's needs, segmenting the target audiences to build advisory boards and recruit mentors who can provide specific and relevant support. Competence in building these relationships will be necessary to engender trust and involvement. Advisors may need to support this process via introductions, vetting advisors and training student executives to manage these relationships. Engaging alumni who live in different cities, states or countries can also create a global pool of people who can bring significant value; however, increasingly multi-modes (e.g. hybrid and virtual) for meetings and communications, may be required to engage alumni effectively.

To develop alumni relationships, it is crucial to give alumni the sense that they are an important stakeholders, adding value to the club's efforts. Their input is valuable even without a direct monetary contribution and alumni are eager to share their experience and expertise, tell their stories and give back through mentor programs, career days, etc. Advisors need to be mindful to assess how student clubs are utilising these human resources once they have been recruited, to ensure that alumni do not become disaffected or disengaged. Keeping alumni engaged requires creativity as well as consistent and effective communication to ensure they feel important to the students and their alma mater.

CONCLUSION

In this chapter, the authors have shown that clubs have a long history. They underpinned the past of major institutions (Clark, 2000). As a mode of learning, entrepreneurship-focused clubs can be traced back to the founding of JA in 1919. As entrepreneurship education took off in the USA during the 1970s and 1980s, clubs grew in both the forms they took and the overall number. This momentum of growth has continued. The 1990s saw the international spread of entrepreneurship clubs to other countries, and the 2000s and 2010s experienced ongoing growth across higher education systems in multiple countries.

This chapter explains why this growth in activity has occurred and explains the benefits of student engagement in clubs. It shows that club growth is driven by a recognition among students and stakeholders regarding the value of clubs for careers and entrepreneurial endeavours. Clubs are shown to assist student learning, enable the acquisition of practical skills and have been shown to impact college attendance, employment opportunities and career attainment. In entrepreneurship, clubs have been revealed to improve student learning outcomes and simulate aspects of entrepreneurial learning. They have demonstrated their impact on student self-efficacy and intentionality towards engaging in entrepreneurial efforts, as well as found to improve employability.

Given these benefits, the authors explore how advisors can support clubs, so entrepreneurship programs can gain the most value from these activities. Many topics of interest to advisors were discussed, including how to support the startup process, how to manage clubs once they are started and how to mentor leadership teams, as well as student members.

Ultimately, the authors argue that revolutionary change sometimes occurs when groups of young people socialise and professionally develop through clubs and societies. Recall the small group of young people in the bar debating and drinking? It might have been the Johnson New Ventures Club at Cornell University, who aims to 'provide programs and resources which prepare Johnson students to launch a company at school or upon graduation' (Entrepreneurship at Cornell, n.d.). Recall the coffee shop example? It might have been a small club founding the first mutual society, the Hand in Hand Fire and Life Insurance Company in 1696 at Tom's Coffee House in St. Martin's Lane London. One of the first insurance companies structured as a mutual society. For 135 years, it operated its own fire brigade and shaped the understanding of firefighting and prevention today (as well as invented mutual insurance). As these examples illustrate, clubs can do more than simply provide learning experiences for students; they can offer a focal point for entrepreneurial change in society.

PRACTICE NOTE

This section summarises the practical recommendations for educators based on the research conducted on entrepreneurship clubs and from our observations of managing clubs previously. It highlights practice issues relevant to readers.

Value and Purpose in Entrepreneurship Education

The research shows that there are many learning benefits for students when they engage in student clubs. They assist the development of practical skills, enhance career opportunities and enable students to acquire critical entrepreneurial competencies. Clubs come in many forms and each form can offer different learning benefits. In practice, student clubs are important extra-curricular tools, supporting student learning in general and entrepreneurship education in particular. As each club offers different benefits, it is recommended that educators and programs aim to strategically support several clubs in entrepreneurship, while also allowing clubs to emerge organically, led by the students themselves.

Managing and Advising Clubs

Our experiences managing student entrepreneurship clubs, show that it is important to actively balance advisor support/intervention with student leadership and effort. There are many risks and benefits associated with student clubs and these must be actively managed while simultaneously maximising student opportunity for learning by doing, experience, learning through mistakes and reflection. Club advisors must carefully counsel about clubs' relationships with university stakeholders, stability and growth, succession planning, risk, while providing mentoring support to student leaders. It is, therefore, recommended that novice advisors first work with experienced academic advisors as they learn how to support clubs and aim to undertake any available training when available.

REFERENCES

Almeida, J., Daniel, A. D., & Figueiredo, C. (2021). The future of management education: The role of entrepreneurship education and junior enterprises. *The International Journal of Management Education, 19*(1), 100318.

Arranz, N., Ubierna, F., Arroyabe, M. F., Perez, C., & Fdez. de Arroyabe, J. C. (2017). The effect of curricular and extracurricular activities on university students' entrepreneurial intention and competences. *Studies in Higher Education, 42*(11), 1979–2008.

Block, S. B., & French, D. W. (1991). The student-managed investment fund: A special opportunity in learning. *Financial Practice and Education, 1*(1), 35–40.

Boone, L. E., Kurtz, D. L., & Fleenor, C. P. (1988). CEOs: Early signs of a business career. *Business Horizons, 31*(5), 20–24.

Brew, J. M. (1943). *In the service of youth.* London: Faber and Faber.

Burggraaf, W. (1997). Management skills from different educational settings. *International Journal of Educational Management, 11*(2), 65–71.

Clark, P. (2000). *British Clubs and Societies 1580–1800: The origins of an Associational World.* Oxford: Claredon Press.

Entrepreneurship at Cornell. (n.d.). Johnson New Ventures Club. Retrieved from https://eship.cornell.edu/item/johnson-entrepreneurship-club/

Evans, M. D., & Evans, D. M. (2001). Community service project planning for ASCE student chapters/ clubs. *Journal of Professional Issues in Engineering Education and Practice, 127*(4), 175–183.

Grinder, B., Cooper, D. W., & Britt, M. (1999). An integrative approach to using student investment clubs and student investment funds in the finance curriculum. *Financial Services Review, 8*(4), 211–221.

Mahoney, J. L., Cairns, B. D., & Farmer, T. W. (2003). Promoting interpersonal competence and educational success through extracurricular activity participation. *Journal of Educational Psychology, 95*(2), 409–418.

McCorkle, D. E., Alexander, J. F., Reardon, J., & Kling, N. D. (2003). Developing self-marketing skills: Are marketing students prepared for the job search? *Journal of Marketing Education, 25*(3), 196–207.

Montes, I., & Collazo, C. (2003). American Chemical Society student affiliates chapters: More than just chemistry clubs. *Journal of Chemical Education, 80*(10), 1151–1152.

Padilla-Angulo, L. (2019). Student associations and entrepreneurial intentions. *Studies in Higher Education, 44*(1), 45–58.

Parkkari, P., & Kohtakangas, K. (2018). 'We're the biggest student movement in Finland since the 1970s!': A practice-based study of student entrepreneurship societies. In U. Hytti, R. Blackburn & E. Laveren (Eds.), *Entrepreneurship, innovation and education* (pp. 146–164). London: Edward Elgar Publishing.

Pittaway, L. A., Gazzard, J., Shore, A., & Williamson, T. (2015). Student clubs: Experiences in entrepreneurial learning. *Entrepreneurship & Regional Development, 27*(3–4), 127–153.

Pittaway, L., Rodriguez-Falcon, E., Aiyegbayo, O., & King, A. (2011). The role of entrepreneurship clubs and societies in entrepreneurial learning. *International Small Business Journal, 29*(1), 37–57.

Preedy, S., & Jones, P. (2017). Student-led enterprise groups and entrepreneurial learning: A UK perspective. *Industry and Higher Education, 31*(2), 101–112.

Preedy, S., Jones, P., Maas, G., & Duckett, H. (2020). Examining the perceived value of extracurricular enterprise activities in relation to entrepreneurial learning processes. *Journal of Small Business and Enterprise Development, 27*(7), 1085–1105.

Rubin, R. S., Bommer, W. H., & Baldwin, T. T. (2002). Using extracurricular activity as an indicator of interpersonal skill: Prudent evaluation or recruiting malpractice? *Human Resource Management, 41*(4), 441–454.

Rutter, M. E., & Jones, J. V. (2007). The job club redux: A step forward in addressing the career development needs of counselor education students. *The Career Development Quarterly, 55*(3), 280–288.

Siivonen, P. T., Peura, K., Hytti, U., Kasanen, K., & Komulainen, K. (2020). The construction and regulation of collective entrepreneurial identity in student entrepreneurship societies. *International Journal of Entrepreneurial Behavior & Research, 26*(3), 521–538.

Terenzini, P. T., Pascarella, E. T., & Blimling, G. S. (1999). Students' out of class experiences and their influence on learning and cognitive development: A literature review. *Journal of College Student Development, 40*(5), 610–623.

CHAPTER 2

SILOS OR SYNERGY? BRIDGING THE BLURRED LINES BETWEEN CURRICULAR AND EXTRACURRICULAR ENTREPRENEURSHIP EDUCATION THROUGH *DIDAKTIK*

Birgitte Wraae[a], Michael Breum Ramsgaard[b], Katarina Ellborg[c] and Nicolai Nybye[d]

[a]*Technische Universität Berlin, Chair of Entrepreneurship und Innovation Management, Berlin, Germany*
[b]*Research Centre for Innovation & Entrepreneurship, VIA University College, Aarhus, Denmark*
[c]*School of Business and Economics, Linnaeus University, Kalmar, Sweden*
[d]*Department of Applied Research in Business and Technology, UCL University College, Denmark*

ABSTRACT

The contemporary focus on extracurricular activities, here the educational incubator environment, accentuates a need to understand what we offer students in terms of the curricular and extracurricular learning environments when situated in the same higher education institution (HEI). Current research points towards breaking down the invisible barriers and silo thinking. In this conceptual study, we apply the Didaktik *triangle as a theoretical and conceptual framing to make comparisons of structurally based conditions for curricular and extracurricular entrepreneurship education (EE). We present a framework that helps bridge the 'what', 'why', and 'how' questions in the two different learning spaces and, thereby, conjoin educators and consultants in*

Extracurricular Enterprise and Entrepreneurship Activity: A Global and Holistic Perspective
Contemporary Issues in Entrepreneurship Research, Volume 19, 15–30
Copyright © 2024 by Birgitte Wraae, Michael Breum Ramsgaard, Katarina Ellborg and Nicolai Nybye
Published under exclusive licence by Emerald Publishing Limited
ISSN: 2040-7246/doi:10.1108/S2040-724620240000019002

possible pedagogical discussions on how they work with the students. The suggested bridge frames a wider 'why' and adds a more holistic and cohesive view of the two different types of settings. Our study contributes to the literature on how to bridge the blurred lines between curricular and extracurricular activities and break down the silos. The framework can act as an inspiration for entrepreneurship educators and practitioners who wish to provide more suitable and sustainable structures and develop a holistic learning environment.

Keywords: Entrepreneurship education; extracurricular activities; *Didaktik*; entrepreneurial learning; incubator environment; curricular education

INTRODUCTION

Extracurricular activities have gained widespread traction in higher education entrepreneurship programmes throughout the past decade (Preedy, Jones, Maas, & Duckett, 2020). There is an increased awareness of their value in terms of practical activities in direct and indirect relationships with curricular courses (Bartkus, Nemelka, Nemelka, & Gardner, 2012). However, the rise in both activity levels and attention from partners outside of universities has come at a cost, namely, the lack of pedagogical development. Contrary to classroom-related EE and entrepreneurial learning (Higgins & Elliott, 2011; Macpherson, Anderson, Trehan, & Jayawarna, 2022) discussions about pedagogical antecedents (Hägg & Gabrielsson, 2019), this seems to be missing in the literature on extracurricular activities. This accentuates a need to discuss potential barriers in terms of what we are offering students in the two different learning spaces under the same roof in HEIs. Further, deeper learning is also challenged by extracurricular activities that do not necessarily lead to reflective practice among students, and, therefore, there is a need to investigate this gap concerning the value of extracurricular activities (Preedy et al., 2020). For example, a study from the UK and Australia (Jackson & Tomlinson, 2022) showed how less than 50% of university students participated in employability-related extracurricular activities, as these were mainly viewed as purely social activities, rather than as activities connected to their future careers.

Thus far, comparison studies that discuss different pedagogical methods have been rare in the field (Nabi, Liñán, Fayolle, Krueger, & Walmsley, 2017), and, moreover, previous research has called for further studies with a pedagogical approach in order to develop and better understand educational perspectives in the EE field (Byrne, Fayolle, & Toutain, 2014; Fayolle, 2013; Gabrielsson, Hägg, Landström, & Politis, 2020; Gabrielsson, Landström, Politis, & Hägg, 2018; Kyrö, 2015; Thrane, Blenker, Korsgaard, & Neergaard, 2016).

Extracurricular activities and the development of entrepreneurship knowledge, skills, and capabilities take various forms, for instance, competitions, networking events, incubation, and an awareness of career options (Jackson & Tomlinson, 2022). To understand one element of extracurricular activities, we focus on incubators as an important service for students (Yasin & Majid Gilani, 2023). Our purpose is to bridge the blurred lines between the curricular and extracurricular learning environments to improve the value of the entrepreneurial learning of the two with the student as the common denominator. To understand the two different learning environments, this chapter turns to educational science and explores pedagogical perspectives in curricular and extracurricular activities, and investigates and problematises the differences in terms of *Didaktik* (i.e. a sub-discipline in pedagogy). Hereby, we contribute to the ongoing discussion on how to understand the entrepreneurship effects of extracurricular and curricular activities in EE (Arranz, Ubierna, Arroyabe, Perez, & Fdez. de Arroyabe, 2017) with a conceptual view of how *Didaktik* can contribute to bridging what risk being silos of the two entrepreneurial learning spaces. The chapter starts with an introduction of curricular and extracurricular, and a discussion on extracurricular incubator contexts. Adding another layer to our theoretical foundation, we present *Didaktik* and the *Didaktik triangle* to make a conceptual analysis of the two learning environments. Finally, we discuss theories on entrepreneurial learning. Based on our findings, we present a framework and suggestions regarding questions to be asked to erase the blurred lines. Our findings reposition the current understanding of what extracurricular entails. The chapter ends with a presentation of theoretical and practical contributions, including suggestions on how to take our findings further to develop this particular research field within EE.

THE CURRICULAR VERSUS THE EXTRACURRICULAR PERSPECTIVE

The first step towards constructing our conceptual framework involves obtaining a deeper understanding of what curricular and extracurricular mean. The adjective form *curricular* with its noun *curriculum* concern the courses offered by an educational institution (Bartkus et al., 2012) and are, therefore, linked to formal learning with its goal-oriented nature (Williams-Middleton, Padilla-Melendez, Lockett, Quesada-Pallarès, & Jack, 2019). The prefix *extra* indicates something outside of the regular curriculum based on non-graded and voluntary activities (Bartkus et al., 2012), potentially akin to non-formal and informal learning (Williams-Middleton et al., 2019). Extracurricular activities should 'broaden the educational experience' (Bartkus et al., 2012, p. 697) which is why we encourage reflection on what is in and out in relation to the entrepreneurial curricular and extracurricular context and areas where synergies exist between the two. We do this by taking a closer look at an incubator as a learning space for extracurricular learning in the context of universities. The development of incubators is part of what previously has been described as universities' third mission, where universities are expected to deliver knowledge and candidates that contribute to utility and economic development in society (Ollila & Williams-Middleton, 2011).

Incubation, from the Latin *incubatio*, refers to a development process, while *incubator space* or *incubator* refers to the physical and structural settings. While incubation is often linked to the promotion of entrepreneurship and start-ups, the concept is *polysemic* (Aernoudt, 2002) and covers private incubators, whose aim is the revitalization of production, regional economic development, and competitiveness through the development of new technology-based firms, which also stimulates collaboration with universities and research and the emergence of incubators in this context (Aernoudt, 2002). In this chapter, we conceptually address the incubator as a place where students can develop start-ups as part of their study time.

Historically speaking, the development of an entrepreneurial university (Etzkowitz, 2013) also entails an increase in the development of entrepreneurial education with a main focus on venture creation (Ollila & Williams-Middleton, 2011). In this development, we see the genesis of a contradiction. Venture creation can be a way to learn entrepreneurship (Ollila & Williams-Middleton, 2011), considering the incubator setting as a *teaching laboratory* where classroom teaching has been moved to practical, action-oriented, experience-based work, learning, and testing in the incubator (Kirby, 2004). However, these two kinds of settings also build on different philosophical starting points, and it becomes a challenge to bridge them, with the classroom representing the idea of 'traditional academic learning, as strongly connected with problem-oriented thinking processes', and the incubator oriented towards 'materialistic pursuits' and 'commercial interests' (Ollila & Williams-Middleton, 2011, p. 165).

Another challenge is the very understanding of the notion of extracurricular relative to that of incubation. A common delimitation in extracurricular entrepreneurial learning is to describe this in terms of activities (Preedy et al., 2020). In a venture–creation-oriented incubation environment, this relates to activities of starting up and running a business with a certain interest in for instance technology or social-driven purposes. In contrast, using the categorical approach, we can arrange extracurricular activities in general as pro-social activities, performance activities, team sports, school involvement, and academic clubs (Eccles et al., 2003 in Bartkus et al., 2012). Relative to venture–creation-oriented incubation, this categorisation includes performance activities, such as competitions, pitching, investor meetings, sales, and the like, while pro-social activities can be part of community events and network gatherings arranged for students and often embedded in performance-oriented programmes, inspirational talks, and presentations by entrepreneurs, business owners, and investors. In addition, we see how blurred lines exist between what is extracurricular and co-curricular, the latter pointing to activities that students participate in 'for meeting a curricular requirement' (Bartkus et al., 2012, p. 699). In the incubation context, an example of a co-curricular activity is students who are doing an internship in their own company as part of their education, but whose activities are outside the ordinary curriculum. It is therefore relevant to distinguish between the two on a continuum ranging from direct to indirect with the following definition: A direct extracurricular activity is one that is more closely associated with the student's major curriculum. An indirect extracurricular activity is one that is relatively unrelated to the student's major curriculum (Bartkus et al., 2012).

This distinction clarifies how extracurricular entrepreneurial learning in an incubation environment can be indirect for some students, such as if they meet a commercial philosophy while being part of a non-business study area. On the other hand, entrepreneurial learning can be more direct with regard to other students' curricular courses when, for instance, a business student becomes part of a commercial logic and commercial-oriented activities in an incubation environment. We see this as an argument for deeper discussions of 'what', 'how', and 'why' learning takes place, which we turn to in the next section, where we elaborate on *Didaktik* in relation to entrepreneurial learning in curricular and extracurricular entrepreneurial settings.

A QUESTION OF *DIDAKTIK*

In the next step towards creating our conceptual framework and elaborating on 'what', 'why', and 'how' curricular and extracurricular activities are used in educational settings, we adopt and unfold *Didaktik* as a theoretical lens. *Didaktik* stems from the Greek concept *didáskein*, meaning to *teach, educate, analyse*, and *prove*. In German and Nordic education research, *Didaktik* has developed as a profession science in the pedagogical field that 'aims at being a vehicle or a tool for thinking about or for reflecting education' (Uljens & Ylimaki, 2017, p. 24). *Didaktik* is based on the Bildung-tradition as 'the initial task of the Didaktiker is to seek the character-forming significance of the knowledge and skills that a culture has at its disposal' (Künzli, et al., 2000, p. 46). *Didaktik* covers the development, examination, and evaluation of theoretically based models for education. It is, for example, used to explore an educational subject 'beyond its definition as an academic subject' (Wickman, 2012, p. 485). Significant for *Didaktik* is that it combines and explores the following questions as intertwined:

- *What do we teach?* (i.e. the content aspect, e.g., the selected learning objectives stated in the syllabus);
- *Why do we teach?* (which can be understood as the goals of the curricula, as well as what the students aim for in relation to the subject); and
- *How do we teach?* (i.e. the mediation aspect, e.g., the teaching methods and instructions) (Künzli, et al., 2000).

It is worth noting that the English term *didactics* is another concept that designates teaching instructions (how), and is as such not considered as a pedagogical sub-discipline (Hopmann & Gundem, 1998). The potential for using *Didaktik* as a theoretical and methodological approach, has been underutilised in EE research (Blenker, Dreisler, Færgeman, & Kjeldsen, 2006; Ellborg, 2023; Fayolle, 2013; Kyrö, 2008). However, contemporary research shows that there is a growing interest in extended use of educational science in the EE field or, as Tiberius and Weyland (2023) express, 'in EE research, the emphasis is not on "education" yet' (p. 145).

Our conceptual approach is based on one of the most fundamental frameworks in educational science: *the Didaktik triangle* (e.g. Künzli, 1998) (see Fig. 2.1). The triangle covers the interdependent relationships between the three vertices of the triangle – the educator, the students, and the subject – while at the same time emphasising the questions of content, aims, and method stated above.

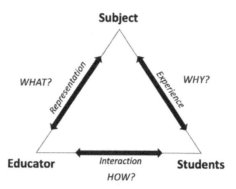

Fig. 2.1.   Our Illustration of the Traditional *Didaktik Triangle* (Inspired by, for
Instance, Künzli et al., 2000).

The double-sided arrow on the educator–subject axis illustrates the educator's relationship to the subject and how the teacher chooses to represent the content. The double-sided arrow on the student–subject axis, on the other hand, represents the students' experience of entrepreneurship and in what ways the content is perceived as relevant. The double-sided arrow on the educator–student axis concerns the interaction between the teacher and the students and how the education is organised. We apply the triangle (Fig. 2.1) as a theoretical framework to make comparisons of structurally based conditions for curricular and extracurricular EE.

In curricular EE, the triangle can be drawn as a subject-specific figure in which 'entrepreneurship' constitutes the upper angle of the triangle (i.e. entrepreneurship is the learning subject). For university incubators, a separate triangle can be constructed in order to explore roles, relations, and objectives of and motivational grounds for extracurricular activities in the incubator setting. In this alternative triangle, we assume that the common objective is not the subject, but rather the start-up or venture creation (Al-Mubaraki & Busler, 2013; Hassan, 2020; Secundo, Mele, Passiante, & Albergo, 2023), and the educator is replaced by an incubator manager, that is, a consultant (Kiani Mavi, Gheibdoust, Khanfar, & Kiani Mavi, 2019).

By placing the two context-specific triangles side by side (see Fig. 2.2), we get a visual overview of the relationship between the two different learning spaces. As Fig. 2.2 shows the students seem to constitute the main common node between the curricular and extracurricular environments, that is, in the current understanding, the students are key in connecting the two learning spaces/silos within the same HEI.

Before we explore this relationship further by using the logic of the *Didaktik triangle* and the related 'what', 'why', and 'how' questions (Klafki, 2000) to review how activities take place in the two different triangles/spaces, we turn to the concept of entrepreneurial learning to assist in creating a bridge between the two learning spaces.

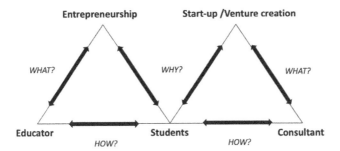

Fig. 2.2.　The Two Different Triangles as Illustrations of Parallel Learning Spaces, That Is, Silo Thinking.

ENTREPRENEURIAL LEARNING

The last step in our theory-building process involves taking a closer look at the contemporary concept of entrepreneurial learning, regarding which Minniti and Bygrave (2001) pinpoint that 'entrepreneurship is a process of learning, and a theory of entrepreneurship requires a theory of learning' (p. 7). The debates have however since shifted towards an action-based and experiential view (Wang & Chugh, 2014), where students, through courses and workshops, are offered the opportunity to experience entrepreneurship by engaging in entrepreneurial work forms or by being entrepreneurs, rather than just learning about the topic (Haneberg & Aadland, 2020). Prior research on entrepreneurial learning has focused on aspects of simulation (Pittaway & Cope, 2007), the entrepreneurial process (Neck & Corbett, 2018), and narrative approaches (Rae, 2000). However, Cope (2005) proposed a dynamic learning perspective to understand three distinctive, interrelated elements of entrepreneurial learning: dynamic temporal phases, interrelated processes, and overarching characteristics. This accentuated the importance of a 'learning lens' and its relevance for general entrepreneurship research and EE. Interestingly, Cope (2003) further highlighted critical reflection and critical learning events as triggers for what he called 'higher-level' learning. It is open to discussion whether incubator settings and extracurricular activities result in a more open approach to these critical learning events and, as a result, have more room to manoeuvre and to expand and challenge the traditional learning spaces found in curricular EE (Cooper, Bottomley, & Gordon, 2004).

As mentioned, Preedy et al. (2020) evidenced how it can be difficult to perform deeper reflection in an extracurricular learning space. Aadland and Aaboen (2018) organised learning approaches into three distinct classes of student involvement: passive, participative (input/output focused), and self-driving (method focused). The latter includes a student focus, making students capable of performing entrepreneurship in different contexts and situations (Aadland & Aaboen, 2018), which resonates with the well-established about, for, and through approach to EE (Hannon, 2005). As such, incubator environments can present an opportunity for students to explore their entrepreneurial learning and to validate their

experiences (Kickul & Fayolle, 2007), but, depending on their involvement, the
processes and outcomes can be very different.

This new knowledge highlights the need for developing the pedagogical perspectives in extracurricular activities and a discussion on the 'blurred' lines of
learning between the curricular and extracurricular contexts. In the following,
we use Fig. 2.2 as a foundation for a comparative analysis of the curricular and
extracurricular learning spaces from *Didaktik* as a theoretical lens.

ANALYSIS AND FRAMEWORK DEVELOPMENT: COMPARATIVE *DIDAKTIK* PURPOSES

Table 2.1 presents our comparative analysis of *Didaktik* in the curricular and
extracurricular learning spaces. The first column in the table introduces the questions that characterise the respective continuum in the *Didaktik triangle* and
the considerations that constitute a *Didaktik* analysis for every learning space
(Klafki, 2000). The questions outlined are then addressed in the curricular and
extracurricular columns with examples of how the contexts have been described
in previous research. The examples discuss EE and incubator activities in general,
and the table can hence be elaborated in more detail depending on what kind of
education or incubation settings are being examined.

Table 2.1. Comparative Analysis of the Two Different Learning Spaces Based
on the *Didaktik Triangle* Logic.

	Curricular EE	Extracurricular EE
WHAT?		
The educator–subject relationship/continuum		
What relationship does the teacher have with the content?	Educators in curricular activities are academics and are, therefore, supposed to have a broad knowledge of the subject (Wraae et al., 2021)	Incubation managers act as consultants based on their own education and/or business experience (Kiani Mavi et al., 2019)
What content is represented and how is it framed?	The content is theory based and is mainly presented through lectures and literature. The content is predefined in a syllabus and usually also includes critical perspectives (Nabi et al., 2017)	The content is practice driven and mainly presented as tools for economic development (Ollila & Williams-Middleton, 2011) and job creation (Al-Mubaraki & Busler, 2013)
What is the aim of the activities?	The activities have a learning focus as they are goal driven and aim to increase knowledge (Hahn et al., 2017)	The activities have a results focus as they are purpose driven and aimed at start-ups (Hassan, 2020) and networks (Secundo et al., 2023; Wachira et al., 2016)

Table 2.1. (*Continued*)

	Curricular EE	Extracurricular EE
WHY?		
The student–subject relationship/continuum		
What are the students' relationships with the subject?	They are formal students who learn about entrepreneurship in order to develop entrepreneurial competences, abilities (European Commission, 2008), and intentions (Nabi et al., 2017)	The feeling of not being a student but rather of becoming an entrepreneur and acting entrepreneurial (Gielnik et al., 2015)
What are the incentives and purposes to participate?	The activities are mandatory and intended to enhance reflection and competence development (Hahn et al., 2017), that is, formal learning (Williams-Middleton et al., 2019)	The activities are vocational (Bartkus et al., 2012) and intended to enhance business development. Knowledge development is based on informal learning (Williams-Middleton et al., 2019)
What motivates students?	Grades and knowledge (Bartkus et al., 2012)	Preparing for a business career (Bartkus et al., 2012) and success
HOW?		
The educator–student relationship/continuum		
What roles and responsibilities are at play?	In the curricular setting, educators are responsible for providing teaching, and, hence, teacher-led processes are common (Piperopoulos & Dimov, 2015)	Participation in extracurricular activities is optional (Bartkus et al., 2012); hence, the students are not there as students but as participants. Incubator managers act as consultants and coaches (Kiani Mavi et al., 2019)
How is the learning space designed?	The majority of the activities take place in traditional classroom settings and are, hence, based on one-way knowledge acquisition (Nabi et al., 2017)	The majority of the activities take place in office- and lounge-like areas (Ali et al., 2020), that is, co-working spaces (Secundo et al., 2023) set up for consultancy work and communication
What methods are used and why?	Conventional lectures, seminars, workshops (Hahn et al., 2017), exams, and mandatory group assignments are common. Guest lectures and workshops are ways to enhance learning	Counselling with business plans and prototypes (Secundo et al., 2023) is conducted in order to develop students' own ideas (Kiani Mavi et al., 2019). Guest lectures and workshops are arranged for inspiration and networking (Wachira et al., 2016)

The *Didaktik* review in Table 2.1 shows that the curricular and extracurricular spaces mainly consist of separate 'whats', 'whys', and 'hows'. From the what perspective, for example, educators in curricular education are responsible for teaching entrepreneurship based on different roles and approaches (Wraae, Brush, & Nikou, 2021), such as a theory-based understanding of entrepreneurship (Nabi et al., 2017), while incubation managers mainly act as consultants based on their own business experience (Kiani Mavi et al., 2019). EE aims to increase knowledge and has a stated learning focus (Hahn, Minola, Van Gils, & Huybrechts, 2017), while incubation activities are purpose-driven and primarily aimed at creating ventures (Hassan, 2020) and networks (Secundo et al., 2023; Wachira, Ngugi, & Otieno, 2016).

From the why perspective, curricular EE offers mandatory activities through which students can learn about and reflect on entrepreneurship in order to develop entrepreneurial competences, abilities (European Commission, 2008), and intentions (Nabi et al., 2017). Grades and knowledge development are presented as a major motivators in education (Bartkus et al., 2012). In a vocational incubator (Bartkus et al., 2012), on the other hand, the students become self-selected entrepreneurs in the sense that they work with their own business development and, thus, practise entrepreneurship (Gielnik et al., 2015) within the context of non-formal or informal learning (Williams-Middleton et al., 2019).

Differences in the two settings can also be seen from the how perspective. When teacher-led processes (Piperopoulos & Dimov, 2015) with one-way knowledge acquisition (Nabi et al., 2017) are more common in educational spaces, the relationships between the incubator managers and students are of a more consultative nature (Kiani Mavi et al., 2019). These differences are further accented by the physical environment, where traditional classroom settings are common in EE and lounge-like areas (Ali, Irfan, & Salman, 2020) and co-working spaces (Secundo et al., 2023) in incubators. Methods such as lecturing, seminars, workshops (Hahn et al., 2017), exams, and mandatory group assignments are characteristic ways to enhance learning in EE. In the incubator setting, counselling with business plans and prototypes (Secundo et al., 2023) to develop students' own ideas (Kiani Mavi et al., 2019) and guest lectures for inspiration and networking (Wachira et al., 2016) are, on the other hand, more frequently used.

The differences outlined above highlight why silo thinking emerges not only in theory but also in practice. However, *Didaktik* constitutes a framework for exploring the similarities and differences. Thus, Table 2.1 represents a foundation for creating a further dialogue between the two learning environments with the goal of erasing if not all then at least some of the blurred lines. Based on the answers that emerge in the table, we suggest a dialogue based on the following questions in order to develop a bridging discussion:

1. How do we create synergy between the practices in our two learning environments?
2. How do we support the students' transition between our two learning environments?

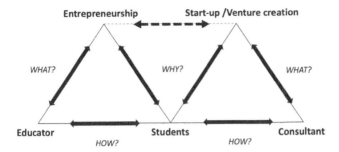

Fig. 2.3.   An Extended *Didaktik* Model Bridging the Two Triangles.

3. How do we create progression for the students?
4. What can we as educators from the two settings learn from each other? How do we create transferability for both students and educators/consultants?

Table 2.1, together with the overall *Didaktik* questions, constitutes, in turn, the foundation of the construction of a new double-sided arrow that connects the EE subject with the incubator's aims, as illustrated in Fig. 2.3.

Establishing a relationship based on *Didaktik* between the triangles, as presented in Fig. 2.3, helps bridge the 'whats' in the two different spaces and, thereby, conjoin educators and consultants in a possible discussion on 'how' they work with the students. In addition, the suggested bridge frames a wider 'why' and applies a more holistic and cohesive view of the two different types of activities that are outlined in Table 2.1.

CONCEPTUAL DISCUSSION

The aim of this chapter was to analyse and discuss the *Didaktik* behind entrepreneurial learning to be able to bridge the curricular and extracurricular incubator learning environments with the underlying purpose of improving the value and learning of the two interwoven learning spaces. We hereby confront notions of what is inside and outside of what are defined as core and peripheral curricular and extracurricular incubator activities. *Didaktik* establishes an awareness of the possibilities of bridging the blurred lines and develops a path to explore how the two learning environments can learn from each other. Here, dialogue questions can help bring the two learning environments closer together and break down silo thinking (Preedy et al., 2020). The questions represent an opportunity to lay the grounds for closer cooperation between the two. They open a dialogue about the value of learning. Moreover, such a dialogue relates to the role perceptions of the entrepreneurship educator, the consultant, and, last but not least, the student. As shown in Fig. 2.2, the common ground is the student, which opens up a discussion on how educational thinking, here represented by the educator, can be brought into the extracurricular environment, represented by the consultant, and *vice versa*, introducing less bounded thinking into the entrepreneurial classroom. Together, these individuals can develop a new way of thinking regarding the core elements of entrepreneurial learning and bridge said learning to benefit the student's education and establish a prepared transition between the two learning environments.

By proposing such a dialogue, we are not suggesting a total alignment of the differences between the two spaces, but rather a more careful investigation of the 'what', 'how', and 'why', which might also lead to more difficult discussions, especially regarding the 'why'. This can be an opportunity to rearticulate important discussions concerning the EE field and questions we care about (Blenker, Korsgaard, Neergaard, & Thrane, 2011) and observe these in relation to actual discussions about the need for the more deliberate use of reflection ('how') in extracurricular learning (Preedy & Jones, 2015; Preedy et al., 2020) or start-up logic/commercial logic in relation to sustainability challenges and green transition ('what'). Based on the above reasoning, the extra arrow in Fig. 2.3 becomes a bridging continuum for direct extracurricular versus indirect extracurricular activities (Bartkus et al., 2012). We interpret the new arrow as an example of an entrepreneurial learning approach that enables students to relate learning *about* entrepreneurship with their own practice.

THEORETICAL IMPLICATIONS

We have introduced *Didaktik* as a theoretical framework from the education field (Byrne et al., 2014; Fayolle, 2013; Gabrielsson et al., 2018, 2020; Kyrö, 2015; Thrane et al., 2016) to explore the blurred lines between curricular end extracurricular entrepreneurship activities. In the extended *Didaktik* model, the students' own work can be transformed into an experience to learn from (Hahn et al., 2017; Haneberg & Aadland, 2020). Transferring value from one context to the other (Preedy et al., 2020) and, thereby, adding meaning to both settings, is a way of increasing students' interest in taking part in existing extracurricular activities (Jackson & Tomlinson, 2022). The new relationship contributes to a more interrelated process (Cope, 2005), with an opportunity to integrate the 'whats', 'whys', and 'hows' from the two *Didaktik* settings. Thus, in a higher-level learning sense (Cope, 2003), reflection is invited in action and action in reflection (Preedy et al., 2020). In doing so, this chapter contributes to the discussions on how the current views of educational settings can be broken down and transformed into holistic learning experiences despite a potential silo thinking mentality (Preedy et al., 2020). We offer theoretical answers that target the invisible barriers between the silos.

The pedagogical awareness of the two different settings can contribute to new ways of understanding the role of university incubators (Wachira et al., 2016). The question of how to define extracurricular activities and their role in relation to curricular EE is still open to debate, but we believe that we have taken the first tentative step towards such a definition.

Our conceptual approach has the drawback that it is only based on a theoretical structural *Didaktik* perspective. Nevertheless, the contribution of this chapter opens up various possibilities for further studies, such as testing the framework empirically. One way could be to observe a dialogue based on the proposed question to understand commonalities and differences in understanding the learning purposes, for instance, by investigating the discourse and language used in the curricular and extracurricular learning environments. Another research direction could explore the roles in the *Didaktik triangle*, how the educational versus incubator environments recruit new staff, and how the two environments 'recruit' students.

CONCLUSION

This chapter argues for a need for innovative thinking within which the educational system leaves behind its taken-for-granted structures and dares to explore and exploit a new paradigm for entrepreneurial learning that, likewise, offers students a new learning experience. Such a bold but necessary move demands not only changes in structures and thinking but also implicit adjustments to role perception. Using the *Didaktik triangle* can be a first step on the way to creating a necessary and valuable dialogue. We believe that our framework can act as inspiration to investigate an underresearched area in the EE field.

PRACTICE NOTE

The proposed framework proposes a practice-based approach to creating a dialogue between entrepreneurship educators and consultants to enable a mutually beneficial learning environment for students. The proposals can act as inspiration for entrepreneurship educators and practitioners who wish to provide more suitable and sustainable structures and develop a holistic learning space that benefits students situated in both learning environments. Further, the questions can start a conversation on how to progress learning, implying that facilitators and entrepreneurship educators from the two different environments need to rethink who they are to be able to provide the right education to students.

REFERENCES

Aadland, T., & Aaboen, L. (2018). Systematising higher education: A typology of entrepreneurship education. In U. Hytti, R. Blackburn, & E. Laveren (Eds.), *Entrepreneurship, innovation and education. Frontiers in European entrepreneurship research* (pp. 103–122). Cheltenham: Edward Elgar Publishing.

Aernoudt, R. (2002). Incubators: Tool for entrepreneurship? *Small Business Economics, 23*(2), 127–135.

Al-Mubaraki, H. M., & Busler, M. (2013). Business incubation as an economic development strategy: A literature review. *International Journal of Management, 30*(1), 362–373.

Ali, A., Irfan, S., & Salman, Y. (2020). University business incubators: A systematic literature review from 2000 to 2019. *Abasyn University Journal of Social Sciences, 13*(2), 499–523.

28   BIRGITTE WRAAE ET AL.

Arranz, N., Ubierna, F., Arroyabe, M. F., Perez, C., & Fdez. de Arroyabe, J. C. (2017). The effect of curricular and extracurricular activities on university students' entrepreneurial intention and competences. *Studies in Higher Education, 42*(11), 1979–2008.

Bartkus, K. R., Nemelka, B., Nemelka, M., & Gardner, P. (2012). Clarifying the meaning of extracurricular activity: A literature review of definitions. *American Journal of Business Education, 5*(6), 693–704.

Blenker, P., Dreisler, P., Færgeman, H. M., & Kjeldsen, J. (2006). Learning and teaching entrepreneurship: Dilemmas, reflections and strategies. In A. Fayolle & H. Klandt (Eds.), *International entrepreneurship education: Issues and newness* (pp. 21–34). Cheltenham: Edward Elgar Publishing.

Blenker, P., Korsgaard, S., Neergaard, H., & Thrane, C. (2011). The questions we care about: Paradigms and progression in entrepreneurship education. *Industry and Higher Education, 25*(6), 417–427.

Byrne, J., Fayolle, A., & Toutain, O. (2014). Entrepreneurship education: What we know and what we need to know. In E. Chell & M. Karatas-Özkan (Eds.), *Handbook of research on small business and entrepreneurship* (pp. 261–288). Cheltenham: Edward Elgar.

Cooper, S., Bottomley, C., & Gordon, J. (2004). Stepping out of the classroom and up the ladder of learning: An experiential learning approach to entrepreneurship education. *Industry and Higher Education, 18*(1), 11–22.

Cope, J. (2003). Entrepreneurial learning and critical reflection: Discontinuous events as triggers for 'higher-level' learning. *Management Learning, 34*(4), 429–450.

Cope, J. (2005). Toward a dynamic learning perspective of entrepreneurship. *Entrepreneurship Theory and Practice, 29*(4), 373–397.

Ellborg, K. (2023). Scientifically based or policy driven? Using a *Didaktik* approach to encompass transformative and critical entrepreneurship education. In A. C. Corbett, L. D. Mario, & G. A. Alsos (Eds.), *The age of entrepreneurship education research: Evolution and future* (Vol. 23, pp. 33–50). Bingley: Emerald Publishing Limited.

Etzkowitz, H. (2013). Anatomy of the entrepreneurial university. *Social Science Information, 52*(3), 486–511.

European Commission. (2008). *Entrepreneurship in higher education, especially within non-business studies: Final report of the Expert Group*. Brussels: The Commission.

Fayolle, A. (2013). Personal views on the future of entrepreneurship education. *Entrepreneurship & Regional Development, 25*(7–8), 692–701.

Gabrielsson, J., Hägg, G., Landström, H., & Politis, D. (2020). Connecting the past with the present: The development of research on pedagogy in entrepreneurial education. *Education + Training, 62*(9), 1061–1086.

Gabrielsson, J., Landström, H., Politis, D., & Hägg, G. (2018). Exemplary contributions from Europe to entrepreneurship education research and practice. In A. Fayolle (Ed.), *A research agenda for entrepreneurship education* (pp. 105–126). Cheltenham: Edward Elgar Publishing.

Gielnik, M. M., Frese, M., Kahara-Kawuki, A., Katono, I. W., Kyejjusa, S., Ngoma, M., Munene, J., Namatovu-Dawa, R., Nansubuga, F., & Orobia, L. (2015). Action and action-regulation in entrepreneurship: Evaluating a student training for promoting entrepreneurship. *Academy of Management Learning & Education, 14*(1), 69–94.

Hägg, G., & Gabrielsson, J. (2019). A systematic literature review of the evolution of pedagogy in entrepreneurial education research. *International Journal of Entrepreneurial Behavior & Research, 26*(5), 829–861.

Hahn, D., Minola, T., Van Gils, A., & Huybrechts, J. (2017). Entrepreneurial education and learning at universities: Exploring multilevel contingencies. *Entrepreneurship & Regional Development, 29*(9–10), 945–974.

Haneberg, D. H., & Aadland, T. (2020). Learning from venture creation in higher education. *Industry and Higher Education, 34*(3), 121–137.

Hannon, P. D. (2005). Philosophies of enterprise and entrepreneurship education and challenges for higher education in the UK. *The International Journal of Entrepreneurship and Innovation, 6*(2), 105–114.

Hassan, N. A. (2020). University business incubators as a tool for accelerating entrepreneurship: Theoretical perspective. *Review of Economics and Political Science*. (Ahead of print).

Higgins, D., & Elliott, C. (2011). Learning to make sense: What works in entrepreneurial education? *Journal of European Industrial Training, 35*(4), 345–367.

Hopmann, S., & Gundem, B. B. (1998). Didaktik meets curriculum: Towards a new agenda. In B. B. Gundhem & S. Hopman (Eds.), *Didaktik and/or curriculum: An international dialogue* (pp. 331–354). New York, NY: Peter Lang Publishing.

Jackson, D., & Tomlinson, M. (2022). The relative importance of work experience, extra-curricular and university-based activities on student employability. *Higher Education Research & Development*, *41*(4), 1119–1135.

Kiani Mavi, R., Gheibdoust, H., Khanfar, A. A., & Kiani Mavi, N. (2019). Ranking factors influencing strategic management of university business incubators with ANP. *Management Decision*, *57*(12), 3492–3510.

Kickul, J., & Fayolle, A. (2007). Cornerstones of change: Revisiting and challenging new perspectives on research in entrepreneurship education. In A. Fayolle (Ed.), *Handbook of research in entrepreneurship education, Volume 1. A general perspective* (pp. 1–17). Cheltenham: Edward Elgar.

Kirby, D. A. (2004). Entrepreneurship education: Can business schools meet the challenge? *Education + Training*, *46*(8/9), 510–519.

Klafki, W. (2000). Didaktik analysis as the core of preparation of instruction. In I. Westbury, S. Hopmann, & K. Riquarts (Eds.), *Teaching as a reflective practice: The German Didaktik tradition* (pp. 245–282). New York, NY: Routledge.

Künzli, R. (1998). The common frame and the places of Didaktik. In B. Gundem & S. Hopmann (Eds.), *Didaktik and/or curriculum. An international dialogue* (pp. 29–46). New York, NY: Peter Lang Verlag.

Künzli, R. (2000). German didaktik: Models and re-presentation, of intercourse, and of experience. In I. Westbury et al. (Eds.), *Teaching as reflective practice – The German Didaktik tradition* (pp. 78–105). Chicago, IL: Earlbaum.

Kyrö, P. (2008). A theoretical framework for teaching and learning entrepreneurship. *International Journal of Business and Globalisation*, *2*(1), 39–55.

Kyrö, P. (2015). The conceptual contribution of education to research on entrepreneurship education. *Entrepreneurship & Regional Development*, *27*(9–10), 599–618.

Macpherson, A., Anderson, L., Trehan, K., & Jayawarna, D. (2022). Entrepreneurial learning: A situated and contextual process. *International Journal of Entrepreneurial Behavior & Research*, *28*(2), 277–282.

Minniti, M., & Bygrave, W. (2001). A dynamic model of entrepreneurial learning. *Entrepreneurship Theory and Practice*, *25*(3), 5–16.

Nabi, G., Liñán, F., Fayolle, A., Krueger, N., & Walmsley, A. (2017). The impact of entrepreneurship education in higher education: A systematic review and research agenda. *Academy of Management Learning & Education*, *16*(2), 277–299.

Neck, H. M., & Corbett, A. C. (2018). The scholarship of teaching and learning entrepreneurship. *Entrepreneurship Education and Pedagogy*, *1*(1), 8–41.

Ollila, S., & Williams-Middleton, K. (2011). The venture creation approach: Integrating entrepreneurial education and incubation at the university. *International Journal of Entrepreneurship and Innovation Management*, *13*(2), 161–178.

Piperopoulos, P., & Dimov, D. (2015). Burst bubbles or build steam? Entrepreneurship education, entrepreneurial self-efficacy, and entrepreneurial intentions. *Journal of Small Business Management*, *53*(4), 970–985.

Pittaway, L., & Cope, J. (2007). Simulating entrepreneurial learning: Integrating experiential and collaborative approaches to learning. *Management Learning*, *38*(2), 211–233.

Preedy, S., & Jones, P. (2015). An investigation into university extra-curricular enterprise support provision. *Education + Training*, *57*(8/9), 992–1008.

Preedy, S., Jones, P., Maas, G., & Duckett, H. (2020). Examining the perceived value of extracurricular enterprise activities in relation to entrepreneurial learning processes. *Journal of Small Business and Enterprise Development*, *27*(7), 1085–1105.

Rae, D. (2000). Understanding entrepreneurial learning: A question of how? *International Journal of Entrepreneurial Behaviour & Research*, *6*(3), 145–159.

Secundo, G., Mele, G., Passiante, G., & Albergo, F. (2023). University business idea incubation and stakeholders' engagement: Closing the gap between theory and practice. *European Journal of Innovation Management*, *26*(4), 1005–1033.

Thrane, C., Blenker, P., Korsgaard, S., & Neergaard, H. (2016). The promise of entrepreneurship education: Reconceptualizing the individual–opportunity nexus as a conceptual framework for entrepreneurship education. *International Small Business Journal, 34*(7), 905–924.

Tiberius, V., & Weyland, M. (2023). Entrepreneurship education or entrepreneurship education? A bibliometric analysis. *Journal of Further and Higher Education, 47*(1), 134–149.

Uljens, M., & Ylimaki, R. M. (2017). Non-affirmative theory of education as a foundation for curriculum studies, didaktik and educational leadership. In M. Uljens & R. M. Ylimaki (Eds), *Bridging educational leadership, curriculum theory and Didaktik* (pp. 3–145). Wiesbaden: Springer.

Wachira, K., Ngugi, P., & Otieno, R. O. (2016). Role of social networks in university based business incubators in promoting entrepreneurship growth in Kenya. *International Journal of Academic Research in Economics and Management Sciences, 6*(1), 1–15.

Wang, C. L., & Chugh, H. (2014). Entrepreneurial learning: Past research and future challenges. *International Journal of Management Reviews, 16*(1), 24–61.

Wickman, P. O. (2012). Using pragmatism to develop didactics in Sweden. *Zeitschrift für Erziehungswissenschaft, 15*(3), 483–501.

Williams-Middleton, K., Padilla-Melendez, A., Lockett, N., Quesada-Pallarès, C., & Jack, S. (2019). The university as an entrepreneurial learning space: The role of socialized learning in developing entrepreneurial competence. *International Journal of Entrepreneurial Behavior & Research, 27*(5), 1264–1284.

Wraae, B., Brush, C., & Nikou, S. (2021). The entrepreneurship educator: Understanding role identity. *Entrepreneurship Education and Pedagogy, 5*(1), 3–35.

Yasin, N., & Majid Gilani, S. A. (2023). Assessing the current state of university-based business incubators in Canada. *Industry and Higher Education, 37*(3), 359–369.

CHAPTER 3

THE ROLE OF BUSINESS INCUBATORS AS EXTRA-CURRICULAR ENTREPRENEURSHIP ACTIVITY IN UNIVERSITIES

Eleanor Browne

Coventry University Social Enterprise CIC, Coventry University, Coventry, UK

ABSTRACT

With practical entrepreneurship capabilities becoming ever more important for all university graduates, whether they are starting their own business or adding value to an organisation by innovating, improving, and problem-solving, what role do business incubators (BIs) play in helping to develop these capabilities for students? This chapter aims to better understand the role of BIs as extra-curricular entrepreneurship activity in universities through a narrative account of business incubation practice in three institutions – two in England and one in Australia. Utilising a practice-led methodology, the study is underpinned by social capital theory and a critical realist ontological perspective on incubation's mechanisms, processes, and structures. Across these examples, there are common underpinning principles of entrepreneurial learning and socio-economic development. However, there are differences in implementation regarding space for incubation. Where the BI is on campus and closely integrated with extra-curricular entrepreneurship activity, this results in a cohesive graduate startup community and ongoing peer support. With no BI present, the opposite is observed. The chapter argues that without the infrastructure to build and maintain a community of nascent entrepreneurs

Extracurricular Enterprise and Entrepreneurship Activity: A Global and Holistic Perspective
Contemporary Issues in Entrepreneurship Research, Volume 19, 31–43
Copyright © 2024 by Eleanor Browne
Published under exclusive licence by Emerald Publishing Limited
ISSN: 2040-7246/doi:10.1108/S2040-724620240000019003

to benefit from sustained peer learning, there can be negative impacts on the entrepreneurs and a visible gap affecting the entrepreneurial ecosystem. The chapter concludes with a practice note providing practical considerations for university BIs in communicating the significance of the incubator peer group to prospective entrepreneurs to improve realistic expectations and potentially improve their reach to entrepreneurs who may be experiencing isolation during their startup journey.

Keywords: Incubator; entrepreneurial learning; peer learning; entrepreneurship; UK; Australia

INTRODUCTION

BIs leverage resources, connections, and know-how to support new businesses that aim to grow and scale, known as 'startups' (Hansen, Chesbrough, Nohria, & Sull, 2000), with the aim of nurturing them into mature, growing enterprises. BIs can provide a combination of office space, business support, network connections, and other shared services to help startups accelerate their growth and chances of success. Typical features that distinguish BIs from accelerators and other startup support services include fee-based rather than equity-based, a rolling intake rather than cohorts, though there is often an upper time limit, and have some selective admission criteria to ensure suitability for support and differentiation from rented office services that do not provide business support (Centre for Entrepreneurs, 2022).

BIs are an established feature of entrepreneurial ecosystems. These are ecosystems that incorporate 'the types of cultural, social, economic, and political environments within a region that support high-growth entrepreneurship' (Spigel & Harrison, 2018, p. 151). BIs can be developed by local and regional governments, private sector, educational institutions, or formed by a combination of actors from multiple sectors (Hausberg & Korreck, 2020). According to the Centre for Entrepreneur's (2022) latest sector survey, there are currently over 400 active BIs in the UK.

University BIs support universities' knowledge exchange activities, functioning as a bridge between the university and the external business community (Grilli & Marzano, 2023), often as part of a mechanism for commercialising research. Universities utilise BIs to encourage and support their entrepreneurial communities to start businesses. Increasingly, an entrepreneurial approach to problemsolving and innovation is applicable to all graduates, and some students may participate in extra-curricular entrepreneurial activities to develop entrepreneurial skills and enhance their employability and network connections (Preedy, Jones, Maas, & Duckett, 2020). In their role as a bridge to the outside, university BIs can be utilised as a part of the university's extra-curricular entrepreneurship education strategy, connecting startups and students. University BIs are considered to provide immersive startup experiences of learning 'through' entrepreneurship (The Quality Assurance Agency for Higher Education, 2018). With new startups emerging and 'live' businesses operating from the incubation space, incubators can provide practical entrepreneurship scenarios that may otherwise be difficult to create or replicate in an education setting.

This chapter discusses the role that the BI and its peer group of startup founders play in the university extra-curricular entrepreneurship landscape. It considers narrative accounts from three universities – two in England and one in Australia – and aims to explore the incubators' place in extra-curricular entrepreneurship education activities, underpinned by social capital theory (Bourdieu, 1986). Consideration is given to context and draws on the literature to ask what this means for policy and planning of incubation infrastructure in universities, contributing to the discussions on entrepreneurial education and business incubation (Blank, 2021; Jones, Meckel, & Taylor, 2021; Mele, Sansone, Secundo, & Paolucci, 2022; Nicholls-Nixon, Valliere, Gedeon, & Wise, 2021; Preedy et al., 2020; Sansone, Andreotti, Colombelli, & Landoni, 2020; Sullivan, Marvel, & Wolfe, 2021; van Rijnsoever, 2022).

METHODOLOGY

This case study spans a total of 15 years of observation and data collection at three consecutive locations, selected through convenience sampling as easily accessible. Immersed in the university and incubation environments from 2007 to 2022, this study describes three universities: two in England and one in Australia. Alongside the many similarities and synergies between these two countries through sharing the English language and their attraction to international students, there are two notable differences in their higher education sectors relevant to this study. Firstly, Australia provides significant flexibility in the choice of courses within a formal learning program in comparison to England. Secondly is the maturity of the entrepreneurial education support networks. In England and the UK, there are several national membership organisations dedicated to the development of the entrepreneurial education sector through professional development, conferences, etc. However, in Australia, this is nascent, and the entrepreneurial education support structure is only just emerging through the more developed entrepreneurship research organisations and networks.

Observation is the principal method utilised to capture day-to-day experiences, conversations, and observations of students, staff, and startups. Also, the institutional practices, processes, and organisational structures are captured through a combination of primary and secondary sources. These include relevant institutional strategies, reports, process documents, meetings, events, network activities, and marketing materials. These materials were analysed and interpreted using social capital theory (Bourdieu, 1986; Lin, 2001) to aid understanding of the practices that impact extra-curricular entrepreneurship education and business incubation activities.

Grounded in incubation practice, a depth of understanding of incubation informs the methodological approach taken, as this context aids the building of theory and understanding (Bhaskar, 1978). Recognising the subjectivity of practice-led research, the benefits of enhanced insights are embraced while maintaining awareness of practice influence and potential biases on findings and limitations.

THREE UNIVERSITIES

Three different institutional approaches are described; a university with a BI at the centre of the main campus, a university with an incubator off-campus, and a university without a dedicated BI space. The descriptions of BIs in these settings briefly outline the strategic approach, physical infrastructure, and relationship with other entrepreneurship activities.

University A is a modern university in England. In 2022, University A has just over 32,000 students, with nearly half of them international. The university has a Community Interest Company (CIC) to support the development of social enterprises and provide extra-curricular entrepreneurship training and startup support for students, graduates, and staff of the university, as well as the wider community.

The entrepreneurship training and startup support is delivered through a programme offered in a range of formats to support inclusivity; a weekend intensive, 1-week intensive, 5-week, and 10-week. The programme is at this time usually delivered in-person on the main campus, with some iterations being offered as online synchronous and is open to students studying at any of the outlying campuses, recent graduates, and staff of University A. During the COVID pandemic restrictions 2020–2021, the programme operated on a reduced level and delivered online only, and so in 2022, this programme is rebuilt from this challenging period.

The entrepreneurship support provides two startup ideas competitions for students and recent graduates competing to win seed funding in the form of a small non-equity grant: one focused on social impact, and the other is open. These are funded by the university and Santander Universities. International startup placement opportunities are provided through the EU-funded Erasmus for Young Entrepreneurs programme. In addition to the training programme, tailored startup support is provided through one-to-one mentoring with business coaches. Both the training programme and coaching incorporate social enterprise principles and methods alongside commercial enterprise. With this approach, all nascent entrepreneurs are introduced to a range of business models and approaches as they develop their ideas and test viability.

University A supports these entrepreneurship programmes in part through Higher Education Innovation Funding (HEIF) and reports its impact through the Higher Education Business & Community Interaction (HEBCI) return. The CIC also earns income through providing a range of entrepreneurship training services and consultancy.

There is currently a small Enterprise Hub space in University A's main campus. The limited size of this space, at just over 100 metres square, limits its use to a drop-in enquiry desk, a small meeting space for startup coaching sessions and a postal service for the university's startup community. Beyond this, University A has a Technology Park adjacent to the campus providing managed office space, specialist environments, and conference and meeting spaces. This Technology Park is often the location for university spin-out companies.

University B is a research-intensive institution, on the East Coast of Australia. In 2018, their students number slightly over 50,000 with one-third of those international. Instigated by the university's Student Strategy, University B is investing in entrepreneurship through an Entrepreneurship Strategy to enhance and strengthen the existing offer with the objective of offering entrepreneurial opportunities to all its students and creating graduates with an entrepreneurial mindset. Their investment in entrepreneurial education is recognised in Maritz et al.'s review of the status of Australian entrepreneurship education (Maritz, Nguyen, & Bliemel, 2019).

In 2018, University B has some well-established but disparate startup and entrepreneurship support activities: a faculty-based initiative running startup programmes for students, an annual accelerator programme on campus, and is well-connected with the local entrepreneurial ecosystem. The main campus is in a district approximately 8 km (5 miles) from the Central Business District and does not have a dedicated BI space. However, two incubator spaces are utilised; one is located 5 km (3 miles) further out from the main campus within a university precinct, and the other is part of a shared BI, close to the Central Business District.

The Entrepreneurship Strategy is spearheaded by executive leadership and relies on support and collaboration with faculties and directorates. Through the implementation of the Entrepreneurship Strategy, these separate extra-curricular startup support initiatives develop into a cohesive offer for students under a new unified identity and are organisationally located within the Global Engagement and Entrepreneurship Department. Two highly popular interventions were developed to raise awareness of entrepreneurial pathways for all students; the annual selection of a Chief Student Entrepreneur and a number of Student Enterprise Ambassadors embedded in faculties. The new activities include a much-extended range of extra-curricular entrepreneurship support programmes and a significant increase in the scale and profile of the accelerator programme and pitching competition. International startup experiences for domestic students are part-funded from grants by the New Columbo Plan, or funded by the university for international students. The accelerator pitch events stream online to a live audience in the thousands and generate startups that go on to further their development in the regional entrepreneurial ecosystem.

University C is a modern university in England. In 2007, their students number approximately 30,000. At University C, the BI is organisationally positioned within the Research and Innovation Department.

The BI began in the context of a local economic development strategy that connects the university with the local authority and regional economic development agency, attracting local, regional, national, and European funding to support the strategic plan. A creative industries' focused BI is one part of a larger 'cultural quarter' concept and launched adjacent to the Faculty of Arts in a new building on the main city centre campus. Its distinct purpose is to nurture the creative entrepreneurial talent within the university and the city, bringing them together as an entrepreneurial community in the incubator. Additionally, the university has a Science Park located about 5 miles (8 km) out from campus on the edge of the city, where university spin-out companies are often located, and which also forms a natural grow-on space from the BI. After several years of creative sector focus, the BI expanded to incorporate any knowledge-based businesses in a range of priority sectors and moved to a new building in 2015. While that change brought advantages of connectivity, it also reduced the distinctiveness of the startup community.

The BI is an open-plan workspace environment supporting entrepreneurs from early idea development through startup and up to 2 years before they move on to the wider entrepreneurial ecosystem. Startup space and services are offered on a flexible, monthly agreement, and subsidised for those still in full-time study and priced to reflect local market rates. This revenue from services forms an important income source and is matched with the HEIF, reporting its impact through the HEBCI return.

The BI has significant strength in nurturing startup peer support and collaboration that enables micro and small businesses to increase their sustainability through collaborative practice and continue to do so when they leave the BI. In 2013, the BI gained national recognition for 'Achievement in Business Incubation' from UK Business Incubation (UKBI).

The BI leads a range of support programmes and activities for the startup community within the university and the city. This includes bi-annual startup seed-funding competitions supported by Santander Universities, entrepreneurship training programmes, startup network events, and access to a network of professional advisors on specialist topics, such as legal, financial, intellectual property, etc.

RESULTS

In comparing these three universities, elements in common as well as distinct differences are found. Table 3.1 shows the types of extra-curricular entrepreneurship education activities present or absent at each university. Core to all three are entrepreneurship and startup training programmes, non-equity seed-funding idea competitions, challenge-based hackathons, networking events, and in-country startup placements. International startup placements and mentoring are features of two of the universities. The expert advisory clinic, providing specialist guidance in areas, such as finance, intellectual property and legal issues, is a feature only seen in one institution. In this comparison, one university does not provide a BI space.

In addition to the activities comparison, the broader setting and context for BIs and extra-curricular entrepreneurship education are compared and shown in Table 3.2.

Table 3.1. Comparing Types of Activity.

Type of Extra-curricular Entrepreneurship Education Activity	University A	University B	University C
Entrepreneurship training programme(s)	x	x	x
Non-equity seed-funding idea competitions	x	x	x
Challenge-based hackathons	x	x	x
Network events	x	x	x
In-country startup placements	x	x	x
International startup placements	x	x	
Mentoring	x		x
Expert advisory clinics			x
Business incubator on campus			x
Business incubator off campus		x	

Table 3.2. Comparing Context.

Institution	University A	University B	University C
Country	England	Australia	England
Organisational position of BI and extra-curricular entrepreneurship education	Community Interest Company, a university subsidiary	Global Engagement and Entrepreneurship	Research and Innovation
Incubator space	None	Off-campus	Centre of campus
BI relationship to other extra-curricular entrepreneurship education activities	N/A	Not integrated	Closely integrated

University A

Observation of the extra-curricular entreprencurial pathway highlights that beyond entrepreneurship training, mentoring, and competitions, there is a gap in the depth of support and engagement with the startup community once graduates start their businesses. The entrepreneurs are not directly or consistently provided with infrastructure and opportunities to maintain their university entrepreneurial peer community, and the students building towards startup activity miss out on closer engagement with a community of graduate startups. As part of a refresh of extra-curricular entrepreneurship services, the startup support offer is proposed to be redeveloped with investment in hybrid incubation spaces and infrastructure for incubation that scales the startup support for graduates and achieves a depth of socio-economic impact critical to the sustainability of the entrepreneurial ecosystem.

University B

As part of their institution-wide Entrepreneurship Strategy, the central Teaching and Learning Innovation Department leads the mapping, coordination, and embedding of entrepreneurial learning in the curriculum, with connected pathways from curricula to extra-curricular entrepreneurship. One example is the use of an asynchronous Massive Open Online Course (MOOC). This popular employability MOOC incorporates entrepreneurship throughout the modules. Student and graduate startup founders provide insights woven into the broader employability content. As well as having a global audience of thousands of learners each year in a non-academic credit format, this MOOC is also utilised in several undergraduate programmes to supplement curricula while subtly raising awareness of extra-curricular entrepreneurship support through case studies.

While the programme side of the extra-curricular entrepreneurship support increases, the physical incubator space is yet to reach its potential. Physical and virtual spaces are utilised for interventions and events to great effect, but the opportunity for extending peer support among entrepreneurs as they continue their startup journey is not yet capitalised on. Some graduates utilise the incubator spaces mentioned above, but there is no clear strategy around this or understanding of the value that the space adds to the support on offer through the extra-curricular entrepreneurship education programmes. As a result, these spaces lack the cohesive approach that work so well with the other elements of the extra-curricular entrepreneurship activities.

University C

Some of University C's curricular programmes are particularly geared towards inspiring future startups, especially in digital art and technology disciplines where modules in model startup creation are run in collaboration with the BI and assist in raising awareness of entrepreneurship as a pathway. The BI also facilitates startup placements and sandwich years for those undergraduate degrees that offer these highly relevant experiences. Many of the BI's graduate startups came from these programmes.

This crossover of students, entrepreneurs, and startups in the BI creates a unique environment where actors of different backgrounds, knowledge, and entrepreneurial experience interact. The entrepreneurial learning among this peer group is accelerated, a distinct advantage for those with the least experience, and is reliant on a willing community of entrepreneurs to share knowledge with those around them. This exposure to the reality of startup processes provides both inspiration and realism to student entrepreneurs.

The connection between startups from the university and the city remains strong, with a consistent mix of both applying to and participating in the incubator. Connections through the peer group and wider startup ecosystem are the BI's main strengths that create a track record of creating new businesses that generate high-value jobs and retain graduates, achieving its main objectives.

DISCUSSION

Reflecting on the incubation practitioner account spanning two countries and three institutions over a 15-year period, it is apparent that each institution's approach is underpinned by common principles of entrepreneurial learning through experience, '… so that the learning journey can become a reality' as described in the QAA guidelines (The Quality Assurance Agency for Higher Education, 2018, p. 21). With a social capital lens on the observations, it emerges that BIs function as bridges (Burt, 2004; Lin, 2001), for students, graduates, entrepreneurs, and the wider startup ecosystem (Shih & Aaboen, 2019).

Individuals move in and through BIs; they interact, develop, evolve, building new connections, and leaving others behind as they move on to the wider ecosystem. BIs form open structures for these connected individuals, supporting their varied, often non-linear pathways. The similarities and differences between entrepreneurs in BIs are strengths of a different nature; close ties form with their peers through shared experiences and shared learning, and loose ties form as they bridge new networks to access new knowledge (Browne, 2021). In this context, the students, entrepreneurs, and wider startup ecosystem each function as networks, between which the 'structural holes' are bridged to aid in the sharing and accessing of knowledge, opportunities, and ideas (Burt, 2004). This supports Grilli & Marzano's (2023) point on the legitimisation of founders by the incubator in their contact with potential external partners '… being located in an [*sic*.] university incubator is likely to be perceived as a much more tangible and powerful signal' (p. 4).

Distinct from many other features of extra-curricular entrepreneurship activities in universities, this bridging ability of BIs mean that a student developing a business idea can work alongside a fully operational startup. That startup forms part of the student's extra-curricular entrepreneurial learning, a safe space for testing and experimenting with business ideas and challenges, with the learning outcomes only possible through the infrastructure investment in BIs. This pipeline interdependency is recognised in Mele et al.'s (2022) study on business idea development in universities, where business idea competitions '…have the aim of creating a stable and quality deal flow for incubators, thus effectively contributing to student entrepreneurship' (p. 12).

The importance of peer groups for entrepreneurial learning in incubators is already established (Ebbers, 2014; Jones et al., 2021; Redondo-Carretero & Camarero-Izquierdo, 2017; Soetanto, 2017). Founders and their peers are significant stakeholders in their co-production of business support with the incubator (Rice, 2002). The startup founders' recognition of the importance of their peer group varies significantly over their time in the BI. Before joining the BI, they are unaware of the peer group's role or significance in their entrepreneurial journey. Once they join the incubator as new startups, they rapidly realise the benefits and learning to be gained from interacting with their peers. As they and the business mature and their experience grows, their reliance on the peer group wanes (Browne, 2021).

All three universities align their activities to achieve socio-economic development and are embedded and contextualised to some extent in the regional ecosystem. However, these institutions display some differences in implementation, infrastructure, and relationship of the BI to other extra-curricular entrepreneurship activities, curriculum, and the wider ecosystem.

Do these differences matter? I would argue that while all university entrepreneurial ecosystems must authentically reflect and address the needs and
opportunities of their unique context, culture, and communities, there are some
established features of entrepreneurial ecosystems without which they do not fully
or effectively function, and peer learning is one of those fundamental features at
the heart of the entrepreneurial learning process. Without the physical and virtual
infrastructure to build and maintain a community of nascent entrepreneurs benefitting from sustained peer learning throughout their startup journey (Browne,
2021), there is a significant gap in the depth and breadth of support for startups
and the absence of a cohesive community of nascent entrepreneurs is visible in
the entrepreneurial ecosystem.

CONCLUSION

An entrepreneurial approach to problem-solving, improving, innovating, and
dealing with ambiguity is increasingly relevant and important for all graduates.
The appeal of extra-curricular entrepreneurship activities is growing beyond
those students who intend to start a business in the near future, and this chapter
sets out to understand what role BIs play in extra-curricular entrepreneurship
activities. Empirical evidence is provided through three university case studies in two countries utilising a practice-led methodology to shed light on this
phenomenon.

Comparing the main features of the universities' extra-curricular entrepreneurship activities and the broader context for BIs and extra-curricular entrepreneurship education, there are many consistencies but two distinct differences.
Even though all three universities have strong extra-curricular entrepreneurship
support programmes, differences emerge in BIs where only one university has a
closely integrated BI, and one has no BI. In the university with a closely integrated
BI, the BI plays a significant role in facilitating extra-curricular entrepreneurial
learning by exposing students to the realities of entrepreneurship alongside operational startups in the BI. Students, entrepreneurs, and startups in the BI engage
in peer support, sharing knowledge and experiences, and benefit from enhancing their network connections through each other and the BI. In the university
with no BI space, the gap in infrastructure is apparent in the lack of a cohesive
graduate startup community and the subsequent lack of ongoing peer support
for graduate entrepreneurs.

This draws on and supports Nicholls-Nixon, Valliere, Gedeon, and Wise
(2021), who recognise that a university's BI is '... one facet of an overall approach
to supporting entrepreneurial activity on campus' (p. 23). This qualitative,
practice-based case study adds to the description of university BIs as critical features of entrepreneurial ecosystems (Blank, 2021; Grilli & Marzano, 2023; Mele
et al., 2022) and contributes to the literature on entrepreneurial learning (Preedy
et al., 2020).

The chapter is based on the observation of three universities. Its convenience
sampling limits its implications and is intended to highlight, through these limited

cases, practices and issues relevant to the sector and can be drawn on for further practice-based research.

PRACTICE NOTE

The practice note for this chapter identifies considerations for university BIs in communicating the significance of the incubator peer group to prospective entrepreneurs to improve realistic expectations and potentially improve their reach to entrepreneurs who may be experiencing isolation during their startup journey.

This study highlights that there is a balance to be found between making entrepreneurs and founders aware of the co-production of business support in incubators and the entrepreneurial learning role that they and their peers play, while not over-promising or over-burdening with expectations.

The following are practical suggestions for raising awareness and setting realistic expectations:

- Informal, 'rapid' startup case studies that are resource-light and highlight interesting aspects of entrepreneurs and their ventures at an early stage in the journey, relatable to diverse aspiring entrepreneurs.
- Utilise ambassadorial roles such as student entrepreneurs to bring diverse perspectives and styles into your communication strategy.
- Invite student cohorts undertaking entrepreneurship activity in the curriculum to the incubator, helping to raise awareness and understanding of the nature of support and maintenance of an entrepreneurial peer learning community after they graduate.
- Include a reasonable minimum commitment to contributing to a peer community of entrepreneurs into the incubator terms and conditions of use.
- Brief your business advisors, coaches, entrepreneurs in residence, and any other incubator staff of the relevance of peer learning for incubatees and their role in enabling it to happen through their contact with incubatees.
- Ensure proper introductions are made for incubatees to their peers on arrival in the BI and ample space and time given to informal, unstructured interaction.
- Incubator 'house rules' on peer learning that are transparent about managing expectations and that staff are briefed to support with any issues.

REFERENCES

Bhaskar, R. (1978). On the possibility of social scientific knowledge and the limits of naturalism. *Journal for the Theory of Social Behaviour*, 8(1), 1–28. https://doi.org/10.1111/j.1468-5914.1978.tb00389.x

Blank, T. H. (2021). When incubator resources are crucial: Survival chances of student startups operating in an academic incubator. *The Journal of Technology Transfer*, 46(6), 1845–1868. https://doi.org/10.1007/s10961-020-09831-4

Bourdieu, P. (1986). The forms of capital. In J. G. Richardson (Ed.), *Handbook of theory and research for the sociology of education* (pp. 241–258). Westport, CT: Greenwood Press. https://doi.org/10.1002/9780470755679.ch15

Browne, E. (2021). Social and commercial enterprise interactions: Insights from UK business incubators. In *School of art, design and architecture: PhD.* https://doi.org/http://hdl.handle.net/10026.1/17297

Burt, R. S. (2004). Structural holes and good ideas. *American Journal of Sociology, 110*(2), 349–399. https://doi.org/10.1086/421787

Centre for Entrepreneurs. (2022). Incubation nation: The acceleration of UK startup support. https://centreforentrepreneurs.org/cfe-research/incubation-nation/

Ebbers, J. J. (2014). Networking behavior and contracting relationships among entrepreneurs in business incubators. *Entrepreneurship Theory and Practice, 38*(5), 1159–1181. https://doi.org/10.1111/etap.12032

Grilli, L., & Marzano, R. (2023). Bridges over troubled water: Incubators and start-ups' alliances. *Technovation, 121*, 102689. https://doi.org/10.1016/j.technovation.2022.102689

Hansen, M. T., Chesbrough, H. W., Nohria, N., & Sull, D. N. (2000). Networked incubators. Hothouses of the new economy. *Harvard Business Review, 78*(5), 74–84.

Hausberg, J. P., & Korreck, S. (2020). Business incubators and accelerators: A co-citation analysis-based, systematic literature review. *The Journal of Technology Transfer, 45*(1), 151–176. https://doi.org/10.1007/s10961-018-9651-y

Jones, O., Meckel, P., & Taylor, D. (2021). Situated learning in a business incubator: Encouraging students to become real entrepreneurs. *Industry & Higher Education, 35*(4), 367–383. https://doi.org/10.1177/09504222211008117

Lin, N. (2001). Social capital: A theory of social structure and action. In *Structural analysis in the social sciences*. Cambridge University Press. https://doi.org/DOI:10.1017/CBO9780511815447

Maritz, A., Nguyen, Q., & Bliemel, M. (2019). Boom or bust? Embedding entrepreneurship in education in Australia. *Education + Training, 61*(6), 737–755. https://doi.org/10.1108/et-02-2019-0037

Mele, G., Sansone, G., Secundo, G., & Paolucci, E. (2022). Speeding up student entrepreneurship: The role of university business idea incubators. *IEEE Transactions on Engineering Management*, 1–15. https://doi.org/10.1109/TEM.2022.3175655

Nicholls-Nixon, C. L., Valliere, D., Gedeon, S. A., & Wise, S. (2021). Entrepreneurial ecosystems and the lifecycle of university business incubators: An integrative case study. *International Entrepreneurship and Management Journal, 17*(2), 809–837. https://doi.org/10.1007/s11365-019-00622-4

Preedy, S., Jones, P., Maas, G., & Duckett, H. (2020). Examining the perceived value of extracurricular enterprise activities in relation to entrepreneurial learning processes. *Journal of Small Business and Enterprise Development, 27*(7), 1085–1105. https://doi.org/10.1108/JSBED-12-2019-0408

Redondo-Carretero, M., & Camarero-Izquierdo, C. (2017). Relationships between entrepreneurs in business incubators. An exploratory case study. *Journal of Business-to-Business Marketing, 24*(1), 57–74. https://doi.org/10.1080/1051712x.2016.1275826

Rice, M. P. (2002). Co-production of business assistance in business incubators: An exploratory study. *Journal of Business Venturing, 17*(2), 163–187. https://doi.org/10.1016/S0883-9026(00)00055-0

Sansone, G., Andreotti, P., Colombelli, A., & Landoni, P. (2020). Are social incubators different from other incubators? Evidence from Italy. *Technological Forecasting and Social Change, 158*(2020–09), 120132. https://doi.org/10.1016/j.techfore.2020.120132

Shih, T., & Aaboen, L. (2019). The network mediation of an incubator: How does it enable or constrain the development of incubator firms' business networks? *Industrial Marketing Management, 80*, 126–138. https://doi.org/10.1016/j.indmarman.2017.12.002

Soetanto, D. P. (2017). Networks and entrepreneurial learning: Coping with difficulties. *International Journal of Entrepreneurial Behavior & Research, 23*(3), 547–565. https://doi.org/10.1108/IJEBR-11-2015-0230

Spigel, B., & Harrison, R. (2018). Toward a process theory of entrepreneurial ecosystems. *Strategic Entrepreneurship Journal, 12*(1), 151–168. https://doi.org/10.1002/sej.1268

Sullivan, D. M., Marvel, M. R., & Wolfe, M. T. (2021). With a little help from my friends? How learning activities and network ties impact performance for high tech startups in incubators. *Technovation, 101*, 102209. https://doi.org/10.1016/j.technovation.2020.102209

The Quality Assurance Agency for Higher Education. (2018). Enterprise and entrepreneurship education: Guidance for UK higher education providers. Retrieved from https://www.qaa.ac.uk/docs/qaas/enhancement-and-development/enterprise-and-entrpreneurship-education-2018.pdf?sfvrsn=15f1f981_8

van Rijnsoever, F. J. (2022). Intermediaries for the greater good: How entrepreneurial support organizations can embed constrained sustainable development startups in entrepreneurial ecosystems. *Research Policy, 51*(2), 104438. https://doi.org/10.1016/j.respol.2021.104438

CHAPTER 4

THE HARMONIOUS ENTREPRENEURSHIP ONLINE GLOBAL STUDENT COMPETITION: AN EXAMPLE OF MEANINGFUL EXTRACURRICULAR ENTREPRENEURSHIP EDUCATION

Felicity Healey-Benson and David A. Kirby

Harmonious Entrepreneurship Society, University of Wales Trinity Saint David, London, UK

ABSTRACT

This chapter presents the findings of an extracurricular online beta test of a competition between students of the University of Wales Trinity Saint David and the International University of Malaya-Wales. The competition is intended to promote the concept of harmonious entrepreneurship and the creation of student-led harmonious enterprises that address the global sustainability challenge and deliver a triple bottom line in which profit, people, and planet are in harmony. It reveals that extracurricular learning can attract students from disciplines other than business and can educate the participants, both staff and students, not just about harmonious entrepreneurship but also how to identify and launch an innovative harmonious enterprise that addresses a sustainability challenge. The test identifies how the competition may be improved prior to its global launch and makes recommendations for students, educators, mentors, providers, and universities as to how it might best be implemented. Once revised and launched the competition will be further tested to better understand how

Extracurricular Enterprise and Entrepreneurship Activity: A Global and Holistic Perspective
Contemporary Issues in Entrepreneurship Research, Volume 19, 45–57
Copyright © 2024 by Felicity Healey-Benson and David A. Kirby
Published under exclusive licence by Emerald Publishing Limited
ISSN: 2040-7246/doi:10.1108/S2040-724620240000019004

extracurricular learning can help advance the delivery of both entrepreneurship and sustainability education in universities and colleges around the globe.

Keywords: Harmonious entrepreneurship; online competition; extracurricular; entrepreneurship education; global; student engagement; University collaboration

INTRODUCTION

The aim of the research on which this chapter is based is to explore how entrepreneurship education can help address the global sustainability challenge currently facing the planet. It does so by presenting the findings of a beta test of an online international extracurricular student competition intended to introduce and implement a systemic new concept, harmonious entrepreneurship, developed specifically to address the sustainability challenge (Kirby & El-Kaffass, 2021). This proposed solution is exemplified by SEKEM Holding in Egypt (Kirby & El-Kaffass, 2022), an award-winning enterprise that 'shows how a modern business can combine profitability and engagements in world markets with a humanistic and spiritual approach to people and a respect for the natural environment'.

The thinking behind it is that the planet is a system and as such is composed of several interconnected subsystems, of which the economic, environmental, and human or social subsystems are perhaps the most significant. In accordance with systems theory, this means that if one subsystem is impacted, the others will be affected. Accordingly, it is not possible to resolve the sustainability challenge by addressing just one aspect of it as has been the case to date. Rather, in accordance with Ashby's Law of Requisite Variety (Ashby, 1968), the solution has to be as complex as the problem itself. This means addressing all of the involved or interconnected subsystems. So, in order to impact the Sustainability Challenge, Entrepreneurship has to produce a holistic, systemic solution that integrates economic, eco, humane, and social entrepreneurship, rather than continuing to implement them separately, thereby producing a triple bottom line business model (Elkington, 1999) in which profit, planet, and people are in harmony. To affect this, however, it is also necessary to revisit Friedman's (1970) doctrine that the social responsibility of business is to satisfy shareholders by 'making as much money as possible'. All too frequently this thinking has dominated both theory and practice over the past 50 years, if not longer. Indeed, the search for wealth has often been at the expense of people and the planet, thereby contributing to the present crisis, if not being responsible for it (Kirby, El-Kaffass, & Healey-Benson, 2022a).

In 2020, the present authors (Kirby and Healey-Benson) founded the Harmonious Entrepreneurship Society (https://harmonious-entrepreneurship. org/) to promote and implement the concept. Since then, the concept has been further developed with the creation of a bespoke educational online course, along with the production of over 140 start-up cases which serve as examples of the concept. Together with the original concept and other papers, these have been the online inputs for a virtual, international inter-university student enterprise competition. The latter is intended not just to raise awareness of the concept but to create innovative graduate-led harmonious new ventures that address an aspect of the Sustainability Challenge. It is intended to launch the competition globally once the necessary iterations have been made.

For the purposes of this research, the 1987 United Nations Brundtland[1] definition of sustainability is adopted together with the 17 sustainable development goals (SDGs) that were developed at the United Nations Conference on Sustainable Development held in Rio de Janeiro in 2012.

THE COMPETITION

While there has been, and is, criticism of business planning competitions in extra-curricular entrepreneurship education (Watson & McGowan, 2019; Watson, McGowan, & Smith, 2014), they have been found to provide a range of benefits to participants other than the development of entrepreneurial know-how and skills. These include access to mentors, opportunity for networking and increased self-confidence, and risk-taking propensity (Russel, Atchison, & Brooks, 2008). It was for this reason that the competition format was selected, coupled with the belief that the competitive structure motivates students to actively participate and fully immerse themselves in the process. This kind of activity-driven, engaging environment encourages better comprehension and retention of principles and ideas. It creates an energetic space where learning is self-driven and curiosity is sparked, a far cry from passive, lecture-based learning. Additionally, in the competitive landscape, students are challenged to innovate and think creatively to solve real-world problems. This fosters an essential skill set for any entrepreneur – the ability to think 'outside of the box', to navigate complex challenges, and to devise effective, innovative solutions. Moreover, as students strive to win (to be competitive), they learn also to create ventures that uphold ethical standards, contribute positively to society, and respect the environment – the competition actively promotes ethical innovation, positive change, and sustainable development.

Additionally, it is anticipated that while the students may be extrinsically motivated to participate initially, they are likely to become intrinsically motivated once involved.

Aim

The competition is intended to encourage teams of university students and their mentors to learn about sustainability and how to launch a harmonious entrepreneurial venture. Each team is required to generate an innovative business idea capable of being transformed into a new venture that will address the sustainability challenge. Participants in the programme learn experientially, acquiring both generic and specific skills. Generic skills include the ability to identify and solve management problems, work effectively in teams, organise, and manage oneself, collect, analyse, and evaluate information, communicate effectively both orally and in writing, and reflect on their learning. Specific skills include identifying harmonious solutions to sustainability challenges, formulating compelling proposals, and executing with support. The venture should adopt a holistic approach, covering economic, environmental, humane, and social aspects. It is vital to uphold Elkington's (1999) triple bottom line of profit, planet, and people, while also targeting multiple UN SDGs. As explained by Kirby and El-Kaffass (2021), the vision for the future of the venture should be based on ethical innovation and lead to positive change and improvement in the economy and society without causing harm to people or the environment. This vision should result in long-term and sustainable development. Furthermore, the venture should meet the Harmonious Entrepreneurship PROSPER requirement of being:

- *Professionally based*: taking state-of-the-art quality measures to develop, improve, and grow the business.
- *Spiritually and ethically inspired*: emanating from a principle of doing good on earth – benefit the environment and the wholeness of the world, ensuring equilibrium and justice and sustaining the initial harmony of the universe.
- *Physically/materially concerned*: supporting improvement in the health and well-being of people and the physical environment, including air, earth, seas, and space.
- *Emotionally rooted*: serving and benefitting the community.
- *Rationally and intellectually based*: creative and innovative, finding smart and novel solutions.

Case examples of the intended types of new ventures are provided at https://harmonious-entrepreneurship.org/.

Structure

The competition operates as a self-directed experiential learning programme, utilising online resources and select on-demand workshops. It echoes the point made by Diaz-Iso, Eizaguirre, and Garcia-Olalla (2019, p.1) that students should engage 'with peers and instructors who can create environments of support and trust'. Participants are encouraged to form multidisciplinary teams of six. Within these teams, up to two members may be academics serving as mentors.

Prior to embarking on the formal stages of the competition, teams are required to undertake several preparatory steps. These include acquainting themselves with the work of Kirby and El-Kaffass (2021) and the publication by HRH The Prince of Wales, Juniper, & Skelly (2010). A fundamental understanding of harmonious entrepreneurship is crucial. This can be attained through the designated online course, which offers an introduction to the sustainability challenge and emphasises the UN's SDGs, helping foster creative, innovative thinking, and problem-solving. Additionally, teams are encouraged to explore the extensive collection of case studies available on the harmonious entrepreneurship website. Registration with the HES competition administration under a unique team name is mandatory. Teams are also expected to attend an online introductory webinar, which not only provides an overview of the competition and the harmonious entrepreneurship concept but also imparts live and recorded insights from practitioners and role models on venture research, initiation, and the journey of student/graduate entrepreneurship.

In *Part 1* of the competition, teams generate an idea for a sustainable business venture and submit a short written proposal outlining how it meets the competition criteria. The proposal should describe the idea, demonstrate how it meets the harmonious entrepreneurship criteria, explain its originality or improvement on existing solutions, consider implementation strategies, identify potential challenges, and provide solutions, and demonstrate the team's knowledge and skills to make the idea work.

Each team receives written feedback on its proposal based on the views of the judging panel and the six teams adjudged to have produced the most innovative and feasible proposals are invited to meet with the judges for further oral feedback before entering phase 2. If the idea is based on an invention, the team must demonstrate that it owns the intellectual property and does not infringe any existing intellectual property protection rights.

Part 2 of the competition requires each team to develop an outline business plan for their sustainable venture. The plan should demonstrate the commercial feasibility of the proposal and identify funding requirements. The evaluation of the proposals will be based on a written document and a 30-minute oral presentation, which includes a question-and-answer session.

The report should include an Executive Summary, which is a one-page synopsis of the business plan. Additionally, the report should provide details about the team, including their experience and skills, as well as their roles in the venture. It should also include information about the business proposition, such as its name, legal status, and a brief description of the idea. Furthermore, the report should outline the competitive advantage of the idea, including who the target market is, and how the venture will generate revenue. The report should also demonstrate how the venture addresses the sustainability challenge, identifying which UN SDGs it will contribute to achieving. Finally, the report should include a reflection on what the team has learned throughout the competition process, including working in teams, generating ideas, understanding the sustainability challenge, harmonious entrepreneurship, and business planning.

The oral presentation should be clear, concise, and comprehensive, taking the form of a pitch for funding. Teams should identify the problem to be solved and demonstrate how the proposed solution will address it. They should also explain the business model and show how the venture will produce a triple bottom line of profit, people, and planet. Realistic financials should be presented, demonstrating an understanding of the associated costs and indicative profit margins. Teams should also explain what funding is needed and how it will be repaid.

Each of the participating teams receives a certificate of participation and in addition the six finalist teams receive a certificate of recognition while the first three winning teams are awarded a cash prize to be used to help launch the venture and are offered a place in a virtual incubator and further mentoring.

OUTCOMES

The competition has been beta tested between students at the University of Wales Trinity Saint David[2] (UWTSD) and the International University of Malaya–Wales (IUMW).[3] Two different approaches were adopted. In UWTSD, the competition was integrated into a business studies programme that required the students to develop a sustainability-oriented start-up project, the lecturer creating the teams. In contrast, in Malaysia, the projects were completely extracurricular and not formally linked to any one programme, the students, from Arts and Science, Biotechnology, Business and Computer Science, forming their own teams. As the competition was part of a module, none of the UWTSD teams had a mentor in contrast to the extracurricular Malaysian teams, each of which had at least one.

In total, 18 teams (71 participants) registered and participated in phase 1, 9 from each university. All of them were single disciplinary teams and all addressed a sustainability problem as required. The written submissions were, in the main, original, and thorough but the judging panel was able to select six proposals, for phase 2, that were both innovative and commercially feasible potentially. As it so happened, 3 were from each institution.

In phase 2 none of the teams requested further advice or guidance and only one reflected in any detail on what the team had learned. Even then, their reflections were vague and generalised. They included such statements as:

> We learned about different elements needed in order to run a business.

> We have learnt that being incredibly organised is critical.

> We also learned a lot more on business terms that need to be planned out in order to start a business.

> We learned skills at a young age that will help us to improve and stay ahead of the competition.

Given the specific instruction that the teams received such a response suggests a lack of student familiarity with the exercise, especially when coupled with the lack of a response from the other finalists. Students are not required to reflect on their learning, and when they do the focus is on cognition rather than skill or competence development.

All of the written reports were very detailed demonstrating considerable effort but were assignments rather than business plans. Similarly, the oral presentations tended to be over-lengthy and did not pitch for funding but summarised the findings. Despite this, the participants clearly enjoyed the exercise and learned from it. Typical student comments were:

> I learned a lot about business and the entrepreneurial world from the start until the end process of this competition. (Biotech student)

> Initially gaining experience was one of my reasons for joining the competition. However, throughout this journey, I found that communication and collaboration between individuals are significantly important to complete any task effectively. (Business Administration Student)

> We learned that a startup or business is not only about getting profit, but also about how to contribute back to the planet and society. (Computer Science Student)

Based on the written and oral presentations the judging panel made awards to the three Malaysian teams.[4]

DISCUSSION

Clearly, the competition needs fine-tuning before its global launch. This was the reason for the beta test. However, the test also revealed some valuable lessons in terms of teaching harmonious entrepreneurship extramurally.

First, one of the initial challenges faced by participants was to understand, thoroughly, the competition's requirements and criteria. It became evident that emphasising the importance of adhering to deadlines and word limits was crucial for a streamlined process. A foundational aspect of the competition was introducing participants to core concepts. This included sustainability, entrepreneurship, and, most importantly, the innovative paradigm of harmonious entrepreneurship. As one mentor acknowledged:

> I have a better understanding of the actual concept and framework of harmonious entrepreneurship and how it impacts society and environment. I believe it shall be applied and integrated in teaching and learning as well as research projects for the students and myself to explore and design more ideas in the future.

Secondly, self-directed learning needs to be managed. Students cannot be capable of diagnosing their learning needs and formulating their learning goals if they are unaware of what needs to be learned. The organisers offered on-demand workshops and counselling, but no requests were received, suggesting that the participants believed they knew all that was needed. Clearly, the mentors can play a role but if they are learning also their contribution is somewhat limited. As the IUMW Dean of the Faculty of Arts and Science, Associate Professor Dr Nurul Nisa Omar, recognised 'the lecturers themselves are exposed to areas in which they may not be specialised given the multi-disciplinary requirements of the competition'. Under such circumstances, it would appear that the programme organisers need to negotiate a learning contract (Anderson, Boud, & Sampson, 1996; Laycock & Stephenson, 1993) with each team to ensure they learn what is required of them. According to one mentor:

> working with the students has made me realise the importance of seeding their entrepreneurial mindset at a very young age, so they can see and plan what they can do .... Personally, I learned how to develop a business proposal and am creating my own template to help others.

Third, the involvement of academic mentors was pivotal. Their primary role was to guide, motivate, and ensure that the students were on track. However, it was crucial that they did not take over the students' work, preserving the essence of student-led initiatives. In the opinion of another mentor: 'the competition allows me to motivate my students by giving them some real case scenario of challenges in achieving the sustainable development goals', while the students recognised that 'without guidance from our lecturer we may have lost track of what was supposed to be done on developing our proposal' and 'both lecturers provided the optimum encouragement, guidance and support in this competition'.

Fourth, the participants benefitted from learning experientially. As the competition progressed various entrepreneurial skills were seen to be developed and enhanced by the participants. These ranged from creativity and problem-solving to team building, leadership, and strategic thinking. The competition became a crucible for honing these vital enterprise competences. Participants were not just theorising; they were identifying real-world problems, generating innovative ideas, planning for implementation, and continuously reflecting on their journey. According to one mentor, the 'students feel motivated to address the sustainability issues since they have great chances to apply their knowledge by establishing their own SDG driven business'. As Confucius said 'I hear, and I forget. I see and I remember. I do and I understand'. According to Associate Professor Dr Omar, the competition 'actually opened up a deeper consideration into how the current module and learning structure is designed and the potential for improving it'.

Fifth, feedback and reflection emerged as pivotal components of the competition. Participants proactively engaged with academic mentors and industry experts to garner insights, which significantly refined their entrepreneurial concepts. While reflection is recognised as vital in higher education, especially in experiential learning and cross-disciplinary, cross-cultural engagements (Veine et al., 2020), feedback suggests that students might not frequently practise this in their degree programmes. This observation underscores the need for organisers to emphasise and facilitate reflection within the competition. As Preedy, Jones, Maas, and Duckett (2020, p. 28) concluded, extracurricular activities greatly benefit from additional built-in reflection components.

Finally, while it is crucial to align the project with the broader University ecosystem, as advocated by Mason, Anderson, Kesel, and Hruskova (2020), evidence indicates that integrating the project into the curriculum may not be ideal. The necessity for teams to have staff mentors might conflict with university degree regulations. Additionally, there is an observed trend where students predominantly engage in activities directly contributing to their degree classification, often overlooking non-contributing extracurricular initiatives. The competition seeks participants wanting to not only understand harmonious entrepreneurship but also to initiate a harmonious enterprise. It is essential that enrolment is not driven solely, therefore, by degree qualifications. The competition's core ethos is to educate for harmonious entrepreneurship, rather than about it and to develop in the participants the attributes of an enterprising person. Both the prize funding and feedback from the judging panel echo this objective.

CONCLUSION

Vyakarana (2016) called for entrepreneurship education to be meaningful and asked 'what is wrong with doing well from doing good?'. The answer is 'nothing' and harmonious entrepreneurship demonstrates how it might be achieved and how it is possible for entrepreneurship to shift from a focus on wealth creation to sustainable development (Kirby, El-Kaffass, & Healey-Benson, 2022a).

Introducing students and staff to the concept, however, is the problem not least as there is still resistance to the incorporation of entrepreneurship education into the curriculum (Kirby, El-Kaffass, & Healey Benson, 2022b).

The competition has demonstrated not just a theoretical argument for the importance of harmonious entrepreneurship, but a concrete example of how it can be fostered in practice. It serves to bridge the gap between theory and practice, providing tangible insights for educators interested in incorporating harmonious entrepreneurship into their teaching. By exploring the dynamics of the competition and the learning it imparts, the study underscores the value and efficacy of such extracurricular experiential learning activities in fostering a holistic view of entrepreneurship.

Specifically, in response to the call from Beaumont, Preedy, Stevenson, and Morrison (2016) that enterprise educators consider how they can attract and deliver entrepreneurship education to students from a more diverse range of discipline areas, the competition has demonstrated that it is possible to attract participants from disciplines other than business administration especially if it is integrated into what Mason, Anderson, Kesel, & Hruskova (2020) refer to as 'the broader University ecosystem'. The problem arises when either there is not an entrepreneurial ecosystem in the institution, or a comprehensive system already exists and has done for some time. In either case, the institution's students may be involved, already, in other, established in-house and external competitions.[5] In many cases, however, the primary focus of such competitions is on the practical outcomes rather than the learning opportunity. While the harmonious entrepreneurship competition is intended to create new ventures that address the sustainability challenge, it is also intended to educate the participants about harmonious entrepreneurship and develop in them the characteristics and behaviour of the harmonious entrepreneur (Kirby, 2022).

While extracurricular interventions may not extend to everyone, it is clear from the results of the beta test that they can help the participating students and staff broaden and deepen their learning as Lipscombe, Burek, Potter, Ribchester & Degg (2008) have acknowledged. Initially, the participants may be extrinsically motivated by the prizes on offer but, on the evidence presented here, once involved they become intrinsically motivated and enjoy learning in a community of 'respect and trust'. However, the outcomes would suggest that the teams should be student led – that they should be formed naturally by the students and not 'created' artificially by the mentors.

Recommendations stemming from the beta-test are for:

Student participants to:

- Grasp the competition's objectives and guidelines, ensuring familiarity with online literature and resources.
- Strategically form teams to encompass a diverse skill set and experience, rather than simply teaming up with friends.
- Adhere to deadlines, consistently delivering as required.
- Embrace feedback, reflecting on the learning journey and skills honed.
- Seek clarity and assistance when in doubt about tasks or procedures.

Educators/Mentors to:

- Ensure their teams comprehend the competition's prerequisites and available resources.
- Promote creative problem-solving, reflection, and identification of learning requirements.
- Aid in devising work plans, rehearsing pitches, and reviewing feedback.
- Support venture launch plans and introduce teams to the university's startup ecosystem.
- Facilitate interactions with the judging panel, joining meetings when feasible.
- Oversee any utilisation of grant funding.

University Ecosystem and Providers to:

- Recognise students' potential to commercialise their intellectual property, introducing policies that support and reward them.
- Offer dedicated spaces for venture development, including prototyping.
- Ensure access to specialised technical, commercial, and legal advice as needed.
- Consider establishing a seed fund dedicated to student-initiated start-ups and spinouts.

Overall, the beta test proved the effectiveness of the competition and suggested areas for improvement and the implementation process most likely to be beneficial to the participants and the planet. It demonstrates that it can attract and deliver enterprise and sustainability education to students from non-business administration backgrounds and that they can learn, experientially, not just about entrepreneurship and sustainability but how to address a sustainability problem entrepreneurially so that profit, planet, and people are in harmony. In so doing such extracurricular activities can be seen to have a positive impact not just on the participants' start-up activity, but their self-confidence, motivation, and entrepreneurial skills and competence as Mason et al. (2020) have indicated. While embedding extracurricular programmes into the curriculum poses challenges, as noted by Pittaway, Gazzard, Shore, and Williamson (2015), revisiting curriculum design to integrate certain aspects could enhance the educational experience.

PRACTICE NOTE

Generic Framework for Setting Up a Harmonious Entrepreneurship Competition

Objective: Begin with a clear and concise objective for the competition. What do you hope to achieve? This can range from promoting sustainable practices to fostering creativity among participants.

Team Composition and Roles: Decide on the size of the teams. Involve academic or professional mentors to guide the teams. Clearly define the role of these mentors. They should act as advisers, not do the work for the participants.

Learning Outcomes: Ensure participants grasp the basics of harmonious entrepreneurship. This includes its principles, values, and how it intertwines with sustainability.

Skills Development: Highlight the key skills participants should develop or enhance during the competition, for example, creativity, problem-solving, leadership, communication, etc.

Experiential Learning: Emphasise hands-on experience. This could involve problem identification, idea generation, planning, and reflection on the learning experience.

Guidelines and Requirements: Clearly define competition guidelines, criteria for evaluation, deadlines, and any word or presentation limits. Provide resources or references for participants to better understand and embrace the concept of harmonious entrepreneurship.

Feedback and Iteration: Encourage participants to seek feedback from mentors, peers, and industry professionals. Allow room for iterative development, where teams can refine and develop their ideas based on feedback.

Creativity and Innovation: While it is essential to provide guidelines, ensure that they are not too restrictive. Allow participants the freedom to think outside the box and come up with innovative solutions that align with harmonious entrepreneurship principles.

Evaluation and Rewards: Decide on how the competition entries will be evaluated. This could be based on innovation, feasibility, alignment with harmonious entrepreneurship principles, and overall impact. Consider offering rewards or incentives that further promote harmonious entrepreneurship, such as internships, mentorship programmes, or funding for implementing the proposed idea.

Post-competition Engagement: Consider how you can engage with participants after the competition. This could be in the form of workshops, networking events, or opportunities to implement their projects.

NOTES

1. The Brundtland definition of Sustainability is 'meeting the needs of the present without compromising the ability of future generations to meet their own needs'.
2. The University of Wales Trinity Saint David (UWTSD) was formed in 2010 from The University of Wales Lampeter (the oldest University in Wales), Trinity College Carmarthen and Swansea Metropolitan University. However, its entrepreneurship education provision can be traced back to the 1980s (Kirby, Penaluna, & Healey-Benson, 2022) and it has developed a domestic and international a leadership role that was recognised in 2022 when it was declared the Triple E European Entrepreneurial University of the Year by the Accreditation Council for Entrepreneurial and Engaged Universities.
3. The International University of Malaya-Wales (IUMW) was founded in 2013 as a partnership between the University of Malaya-Wales and the University of Wales. It awards dual degrees of IUMW and UWTSD and it is committed to developing students who are ready to contribute to the next industrial revolution. Its former Vice Chancellor, Tay Kay Luan, is the author of 'Applying Sustainability: Principles and Practices' (Partridge Publishing, Singapore, 2019).

4. The three Malaysian teams were:
   a. *Agropro* – this is an app-based business that is free to use which helps people at home and peasant farmers to build a sustainable farm.
   b. *Hands of Angels* – a business app that tracks survivors of floods and other natural disasters who are trapped or cut off from safety.
   c. *Miracle Makers* – replaces the existing inefficient, large-scale food production system by producing and distributing cost-efficient and environmentally friendly fresh microgreens and mushrooms to people living in urban areas in quantities that help reduce household food waste.
5. Numerous competitions exist but particularly Enactus and The Hult Prize are noteworthy. The mission of Enactus is to 'engage the next generation of entrepreneurial leaders to use innovation and business principles to improve the world' (Enactus, 2023), while The Hult Prize 'challenges young people around the world to solve the planet's most pressing issues through social entrepreneurship' (Hult Prize Foundation, 2021).

ACKNOWLEDGEMENTS

The authors would like to thank Professor Kathryn Penaluna (PhD) of the University of Wales Trinity Saint David and Kay Luan Tay, former Vice Chancellor of the International University of Malaya-Wales, for their support.

REFERENCES

Anderson, G., Boud, D., & Sampson, J. (1996). *Learning contracts: A practical guide*. London: Routledge.

Ashby, W. R. (1968). Variety, constraint, and the law of requisite variety. In W. Buckley (Ed.), *Modern systems research for the behavioural scientist*. Chicago, IL: Aldine Publishing Co.

Beaumont, E., Preedy, S., Stevenson, S., & Morrison, J. (2016). Extracurricular enterprise activities in HE. Students' perceptions of their entrepreneurial behaviours, competencies and capability. Presented at the 39th Institute for Small Business and Entrepreneurship Conference, October 26–28, Paris (University of Gloucestershire Post Print).

Diaz-Iso, A., Eizaguirre, A., & Garcia-Olalla, A. (2019). Extracurricular activities in higher education and the promotion of reflective learning for sustainability. *Sustainability*, *11*(4521), 1–18.

Elkington, J. (1999). Cannibals with forks: The triple bottom line of 21st century business. Oxford: Capstone.

Enactus. (2023). Enactus global. Retrieved from https://enactus.org/

Friedman, M. (1970). The social responsibility of business is to increase its profits. *New York Times*, September 13, pp. 122–126.

HRH The Prince of Wales, Juniper, T., & Skelly, I. (2010). *Harmony: A new way of looking at our world*. London: HarperCollins.

Hult Prize Foundation. (2021). About us. Retrieved from https://www.hultprize.org/about-us

Kirby, D. A. (2022). Developing the harmonious venture: A new approach to sustainability. In K. Penaluna, C. Jones, & A. Penaluna (Eds.), *How to develop entrepreneurial graduates, ideas and ventures: Designing an Imaginative Entrepreneurship Program*. Cheltenham: Edward Elgar.

Kirby, D. A., & El-Kaffass, I. (2021). Harmonious entrepreneurship – A new approach to the challenge of global sustainability. *The World Journal of Entrepreneurship, Management and Sustainable Development*, *17*(4), 846–855. https://doi.org/10.1108/WJEMSD-09-2020-0126

Kirby, D. A., & El-Kaffass, I. (2022). The characteristics of a green, innovative and transformational entrepreneur: An example of transformative entrepreneurship in an efficiency-driven economy. *International Journal of Technological Learning, Innovation and Development*, *14*(1/2), 7–22.

Kirby, D. A., El-Kaffass, I., & Healey-Benson, F. (2022a). Harmonious entrepreneurship: Evolution from wealth creation to sustainable development. *Journal of Management History, 28*(4), 514–529. https://doi.org/10.1108/JMH-11-2021-0060

Kirby, D. A., El-Kaffass, I., & Healey Benson, F. (2022b, April 1). Integrating harmonious entrepreneurship into the curriculum: Addressing the sustainability grand challenge. In K. A. Gamage & N. Gunawardhana (Eds.), *The Wiley handbook of sustainability in higher education learning and teaching* (pp. 207–220). London: Wiley-Blackwell.

Kirby, D. A., Penaluna, K., & Healey-Benson, F. (2022). 40 Years of Entrepreneurship Education UWTSD. *The South Wales Business Review, 9*(1), 1–25.

Laycock, M., & Stephenson, J. (1993). *Using learning contracts in higher education.* London: Routledge.

Lipscombe, B. P., Burek, C., Potter, J. A., Ribchester, C., & Degg, M. R. (2008). An overview of sustainable development interventions in universities. *International Journal of Sustainability in Higher Education, 8*(3), 222–234.

Mason, C., Anderson, M., Kesel, T., & Hruskova, M. (2020). Promoting student enterprise: Reflections on a university start-up programme. *Local Economy, 35*(1), 68–79.

Pittaway, L., Gazzard, J., Shore A., & Williamson, T. (2015). Student clubs: Experiences in entrepreneurial learning. *Entrepreneurship and Regional Development, 27*(3–4), 127–153.

Preedy, S., Jones, P., Maas G., & Duckett, H. (2020). Examining the perceived value of extracurricular enterprise activities in relation to entrepreneurial learning processes. *Journal of Small Business and Enterprise Development, 27*(7), 1085–1105.

Russel, R., Atchison, M., & Brooks, R. (2008). Business plan competitions in tertiary institutions: Encouraging entrepreneurship education. *Journal of Higher Education Policy and Management, 30*(2), 123–138.

Tay, K. L. (2019). *Applying Sustainability: Principles and Practices.* Singapore: Partridge Publishing.

Veine, S., Anderson, M. K., Andersen, N. H., Espenes, T. C., Soyland, T. B., Wallin, P., & Reams, J. (2020). Reflection as a core student learning activity in higher education – Insights from nearly two decades of academic development. *International Journal for Academic Development, 25*(2), 147–161.

Vyakarnam, S. (2016). We need entrepreneurship that is meaningful. *Cranfield University Business Growth Programme Blog.*

Watson, K., McGowan, P., & Smith, P. (2014). Extracurricular business planning competitions; challenging assumptions. *Industry and Higher Education. 28*(6), 411–415.

Watson, K., & McGowan, P. (2019). Rethinking competition-based entrepreneurship education in higher education institutions. Towards an effectuation-informed coopetition model. *Education + Training, 62*(1), 31–46.

CHAPTER 5

ENTERPRISE EDUCATION THROUGH EXTRACURRICULAR CLIENT PROJECTS: THE TRANSDISCIPLINARY BUSINESS CHALLENGE WEEK

Paul J. Jackson[a], Nicolette Michels[a], Jonathan Louw[a], Lucy Turner[b] and Andrea Macrae[c]

[a]Oxford Brookes University Business School, Headington, Oxford
[b]Faculty of Technology, Design and Environment, Oxford Brookes University, Headington, Oxford
[c]Faculty of Humanities and Social Sciences, Oxford Brookes University, Headington, Oxford

ABSTRACT

This chapter contributes to the scholarship of teaching and learning in extracurricular enterprise and entrepreneurship education. It draws on research from two annual 'Business Challenge Weeks' (BCW) held at Oxford Brookes University in 2021 and 2022, in which teams of postgraduate students from three faculties worked on external client projects, supported by an academic mentor. It presents and discusses findings derived from a survey and interviews conducted after the second of these years. The chapter takes a transdisciplinary perspective, after Budwig and Alexander (2020), Piaget (1972) and Klein et al. (2001) and explores the relationship between this and the enterprise and entrepreneurship development pipeline set out by QAA (2018). It analyses the experiences of the three main participating groups engaged in the challenge weeks – students, external clients and academic mentors – and

Extracurricular Enterprise and Entrepreneurship Activity: A Global and Holistic Perspective
Contemporary Issues in Entrepreneurship Research, Volume 19, 59–79
Copyright © 2024 by Paul J. Jackson, Nicolette Michels, Jonathan Louw, Lucy Turner and Andrea Macrae
Published under exclusive licence by Emerald Publishing Limited
ISSN: 2040-7246/doi:10.1108/S2040-724620240000019005

explores the organising challenges inherent in multiparty pedagogical initiatives. The chapter contributes to knowledge in this area by revealing and reflecting on the motivations and expectations of the three participant groups, the roles they played during the week and the outcomes they reported. It also expands understanding of transdisciplinary enterprise pedagogy.

Keywords: Transdisciplinary enterprise; extracurricular; business challenge; postgraduate students; entrepreneurship education; client projects

INTRODUCTION

As universities expand their enterprise and entrepreneurship education provision, a growth of both experiential learning and extracurricular activity is evident (Hyams-Ssekasi & Caldwell, 2018; Preedy, Jones, Maas, & Duckett, 2020). This chapter contributes to the scholarship of teaching and learning in this area by evaluating the findings from two annual Business Challenge Weeks (BCWs). It focuses on the transdisciplinary nature of these weeks and the experiences of and impacts on, the students, external clients and academic mentors who collaborated as part of the BCWs. The chapter also explores the challenges inherent in multiparty pedagogical initiatives and considers how the lessons from them extend our understanding of what are valuable but still evolving learning activities.

OUTLINE OF THE BCW INTERVENTION

The BCW – conducted online in 2021, and in hybrid form in 2022 – is extracurricular and voluntary, and aimed at the University's taught master's students. It provides opportunities for practical business problem-solving and relationship-building: teams work on projects supplied by external clients, supported by an academic mentor. The BCW typically provides four intensive working days, leading to a fifth day of student 'showcase' presentations to mentors and clients, with external judges and prize-giving. The initiative is led by the University's Business School with the faculties of Technology, Design and Environment and of Humanities and Social Sciences joining in 2021 and 2022, respectively. Postgraduate students are recruited to participate voluntarily, outside the normal semester period, via calls circulated by Programme Leaders in these faculties. Students (up to five per client team, from across different faculties) and mentors are thus drawn from multiple disciplinary areas – from finance and marketing, to creative writing and computing. Clients also represent diverse sectors, including education and manufacturing, hospitality and food service. The result has been a transdisciplinary, hackathon-type experiential learning process designed to enhance student employability, enterprise and entrepreneurial mindset (Preedy et al., 2020; QAA, 2018), giving students real-world enterprise experience while also providing value to external clients.

Organisations are explicitly invited to offer a challenge that a multidisciplinary team of postgraduate students can work on for a week, with the expectation of some meaningful problem-solving and idea generation. The external website that promotes the BCW to prospective clients clarifies that outputs will depend upon the challenge, but that they typically include: a thorough analysis of the problem or opportunity; background research and fact-finding; a solution or action plan; and a short report on findings and recommendations. Following expressions of interest, the BCW organising team assesses client suitability in terms of the BCW's focus on enterprise competencies, the need for a range of scenarios to engage a variety of student profiles, and practical considerations such as client availability. Mentors then support accepted organisations in refining and clarifying their project briefs to ensure that these align with the BCW's pedagogic priorities. BCW challenges have included:

- A local fashion studio, seeking ideas on a market analysis and marketing plan, including ways of bringing a new product to market.
- A networking and coaching partnership, aimed particularly at women, looking for advice on business expansion.
- A manufacturer of light-powered sensors for building management, looking for analysis of new markets and new applications for its technology.
- A customer experience consultancy, wanting to test and refine its tool for understanding customer journeys.
- A major Oxford museum, looking to analyse and report on its environmental sustainability initiatives.

The BCW initiative is a targeted intervention within the important contemporary context of 'wicked problems' (Morrissey & Baldry, 2022; Norton & Penaluna, 2022b). It addresses the entrepreneurial mindset, behaviours and competencies graduates will need in the future – namely, flexibility, creativity, complex problem-solving, ideation and adaptability. More specifically, it responds to the challenge posed by Norton and Penaluna (2022b) as to how Universities can develop

> enterprise and entrepreneurship beyond the walls or the confines of certain discipline subjects creating connectivity across the curriculum, ensuring that these aspects are drawn out and defined in learning outcomes, through assessment, through multifaceted ways of recording and reflecting on these skills, and engaging stakeholders in multiple contexts to provide that 'future proofing' that is necessary, and arguably, our responsibility. (p. 4)

A competency framework informs the planning and identifies skills in four core areas: problem-solving, working with clients, team working and personal competencies. These areas draw together key features associated with the 'pipeline for development', from 'entrepreneurial mindset' to 'entrepreneurial capability', as conceptualised by the QAA (2018). This includes learning activities that are group-based, involve projects such as business start-up opportunities or new service design, and engage with external client organisations (p. 19).

The BCW is characterised by three intersecting dimensions: firstly, experiential learning related to future employability (e.g. Dalrymple, Macrae, Pal, & Shipman, 2021); secondly, extracurricular intra- and entrepreneurial practices (e.g. de Greef, Post, Vink, & Wenting, 2017; Norton & Penaluna, 2022a); and thirdly, transdisciplinary collaboration, involving students, clients and mentors together navigating multistakeholder needs and expectations (e.g. Beresford & Michels, 2016). The BCW sits at the advanced end of the education 'pipeline', in which students engage in various challenging learning activities that build and sharpen their entrepreneurial and enterprise effectiveness (QAA, 2018). The BCW initiative also draws on Budwig and Alexander's (2020) 'developmental' view of the student as an emerging adult, and aligns with their emphasis on the importance of leadership groups within the University in fashioning learning environments. Following Budwig and Alexander (2020) and Piaget (1972), the BCW is positioned as transdisciplinary, because it places 'relationships within a total system without any boundaries between disciplines' (Piaget, 1972, p. 138), enabling participants to exhibit agency and collaborate in activities that transcend disciplinary divisions and discipline-based learning outcomes or criteria. Additionally, working with external clients to solve real-world problems inevitably entails transdisciplinarity (Klein et al., 2001). Lees, Djordjevic and Roberts (2022) and Morrissey and Baldry (2022) have explored student perceptions and outcomes linked to employability skills in multidisciplinary settings. The latter authors note the importance of interdisciplinary problem-solving as central to preparing students for the societal and global changes they will meet in the workplace (Morrissey & Baldry, 2022, p. 9).

The BCW takes team-based creative problem-solving beyond student peer transdisciplinary teams by also involving academic staff (as mentors) and external partners (as project clients) in the learning experience, responding to Budwig and Alexander's (2020) additional call for 'students and faculty to work collaboratively with other units on campus, and for universities to build partnerships beyond the campus gates' (p. 10). However, such an approach entails complexities in academic mentors, students with different disciplinary backgrounds, and clients finding a shared, meaningful and inclusive language as well as shared practices through which to articulate and enact enterprising competencies.

For these and other reasons, the BCW can be located in the 'liminoid' (Turner, 1974) space of enterprise education (Gaggiotti, Jarvis, & Richards, 2020). The BCW involves greater levels of risk-taking, innovation, creativity and uncertainty than traditional, in-curricular pedagogy. Participants – mentors, clients and students – all face unpredictable circumstances, lacking in familiarity and security. The BCW, for instance, requires staff to undertake enterprise mentoring in the context of student work with external businesses – often with the students and client problems coming from disciplines far removed from their own. This may go beyond mentors' regular roles, leading to experiences at the edges of their expertise and feelings of confidence. For client organisations, working with universities and their students also involves novelty and uncertainty, as well as the potential start of inter-institutional relationships. For students, too, working with people from different disciplines in an intensive week-long structure, together with external organisations and academic mentors, is also far removed from the familiar, liminal end of the enterprise education continuum (Spiegel, 2011).

The following sections describe the data collection that has followed the BCWs, and present and reflect on findings in the context of current scholarship.

DATA COLLECTION AND FINDINGS

Data Collection and Summary

Some 50 students completed the BCW across 2021 and 2022, with roughly 8 clients and 8 mentors involved in each year. Following both BCWs, students and clients were surveyed. In 2021, 14 students and 5 clients completed surveys. In 2022, the mentors were also included in the survey, and 8 interviews were conducted with 3 mentors, 3 clients and 2 students. This account draws principally on the 2022 data, as the surveys were more comprehensive than in 2021, the interviews were added and mentors were included.

The 2022 survey was completed by 22 people (equating to roughly 50% of each cohort: 13 students, 5 clients and 4 mentors). Data from the 8 interviews in 2022 were transcribed and then analysed using NVivo. Initial coding of the interview data revealed high-level themes around participant motivations, reported outcomes and benefits, perceptions of participant roles, and suggestions for future BCWs. A second round of coding produced a range of sub-themes.

Table 5.1 presents a summary of the quantitative survey data. The survey also invited students, mentors and clients to answer open questions. These same questions were further explored by those survey respondents who additionally volunteered to be interviewed. Students were asked about: motivations to take part in the BCW; how the extracurricular nature of the BCW affected their

Table 5.1. Summary of 2022 Quantitative Survey Data.

Summary of Quantitative Survey Data (Mentor Data From Survey Was Qualitative Only)

Students ($n = 13$)			
How was your experience of …	Poor	Neutral	Positive
… the week in general?	0	2	11
… working with your client?	0	2	11
… working with your fellow team members?	3	3	7
… working with your University mentor?	1	0	12
How far did the BCW provide the opportunity to practise and enhance your …	Not at all	A Little	A Lot
… problem-solving skills	0	5	8
… skills in working with clients	1	4	8
… team working skills	1	4	8
… skills in working with students from other subject areas	0	6	7
… personal resilience skills	0	4	9
… presentation skills	0	5	8
… self-awareness skills	0	6	7
Clients ($n = 5$)			
How was your experience of …	Poor	Neutral	Positive
… working with the students?	1	1	3
… working with your University mentor?	1	1	3
… working with the organising team?	0	1	4
… working with the University as a partner?	0	1	4

experience and motivation to take part; and what the BCW organising team could have done better prior to and during the BCW. Mentors (who are not included in Table 5.1 as they were asked only open-text questions) were asked about: their motivations to take part in the BCW; their experiences of working with the BCW organising team, students and clients; the likelihood of their participation as a mentor the following year; and what more the University could do to support initiatives like the BCW. Clients were asked about: their motivations to take part in the BCW; the practical outcomes of the BCW for them and their organisation and what value this provided; how far their expectations of the BCW were met, and what could have been done differently if their expectations were not fully met. Clients were also provided with a space to provide any further comments.

Table 5.2 presents a summary of the themes and subthemes arising from the open survey questions and also from the interview data. The following section then presents a more detailed discussion and evaluation of these findings in terms of implications for practice and wider literature on enterprise education.

Table 5.2.   Summary of Themes Arising From 2022 Open Survey Questions and From Interview Data.

Summary of Themes Arising From Open Survey Questions and From Interview Data	
Theme 1: Motivations	
Students	(1) Exposure to real-world people and organisations
	(2) Interest in other university disciplines
	(3) Desire for a challenge
Clients	(1) Search for new ideas and fresh eyes
	(2) Opportunity to foster University links
	(3) Offering an experience of value to students
Mentors	(1) Intrinsic interest in working with students on projects
	(2) Recognition of the value of the initiative to students
	(3) Extracurricular nature of the BCW
	(4) Influence of colleagues and managers
	(5) Personal benefits from external engagement
Theme 2: Perceived Outcomes	
Students	(1) Benefits of team working
	(2) Building relationships with clients
	(3) Being tested and challenged
	(4) Developing self-confidence
	(5) Having a story to tell employers
	(6) Exposure to people from different cultures
	(7) Self-understanding
Clients	(1) New ideas and insights
	(2) Impartial feedback
	(3) Adding to the impetus for change
Mentors	(1) Being part of a mentor community
	(2) Positive experience of collaborative problem-solving with students
	(3) Desire to continue as a mentor

Table 5.2. *(Continued)*

Summary of Themes Arising From Open Survey Questions and From Interview Data

Theme 3: Perceptions of Roles	
Students	(1) Team member
	(2) Individual strengths and weaknesses in team role
	(3) Reliance on mentor for confidence building
	(4) Reliance on mentor to facilitate playing to strengths
	(5) Reliance on mentor for supporting networking
	(6) Reliance on client for support
	(7) Reliance on client for support with team building
Clients	(1) A mutual exchange of value
	(2) A willingness to experiment
	(3) The importance of the client role in fostering a good student-client relationship
	(4) Clients as potential mentors
	(5) Recognising the value of team diversity
	(6) Recognising reputation of university and students
	(7) Expectations regarding role of academic mentor
Mentors	(1) Recognition of the work commitment alongside regular role
	(2) Freedom from bureaucracy involved in regular role
	(3) Mentor role ambiguity
	(4) Generic mentoring skills
	(5) Team versus individual mentor
	(6) Providing students with 'reality check'
	(7) Help students reflect on learning
	(8) Connecting with real world practice beyond regular role
Theme 4: Recommendations for Future Practice	
Students	(1) Better communication
Clients	(1) Better communication
	(2) Clarity about client eligibility
	(3) Clarity about potential value for the client
	(4) Orientating the client
	(5) Managing the client
	(6) Planning ahead of the week
Mentors	(1) Better communication
	(2) Orientating the client
	(3) Managing the client
	(4) Transparency regarding required level of commitment
	(5) Planning ahead of the week
	(6) Alignment of extracurricular activity alongside in-curricular activity

MOTIVATIONS OF PARTICIPANTS

The data showed a range of mutually supporting motivations among the respondents in their BCW roles as students, clients or mentors.

Student Motivations

For the students, three key drivers (themes) emerged from the interviews and survey data: (1) interest in exposure to real-world people and organisations; (2) interest in other disciplines and approaches; and (3) a desire for a challenge.

While some of the students had previous work experience, most had none. International students, including those with prior work experience, saw engaging with the UK environment beyond the University as appealing. The opportunity to learn something outside the classroom and gain 'real exposure to how other people work' (Student 1) was a particular spur (theme 1). This included the opportunity to develop new skills and apply degree-based learning – and to do this in a way that offered value to the clients.

The framing of the week as a transdisciplinary initiative was clearly attractive to some students. This revealed an interest in other programmes and university departments (theme 2), with the likelihood that insights into different parts of the University, and links with other students, would emerge from the week. Student 1 noted, for instance, 'I was pretty interested in how other people on different postgraduate courses work'.

For some, the very idea of a 'challenge' resonated (theme 3). The same interviewee (Student 1) commented, 'I just wanted to kind of challenge myself', noting that, 'following my MA, I'm going to have to really challenge myself within the workplace'. Student 2 noted how their 'expectations were really high' with regard to how demanding the experience would be. These responses add new understanding to the QAA pipeline concept, particularly in terms of 'mindset'. We can argue, for instance, that students in this extracurricular context do not simply have an evolving sense of themselves as creative and resourceful learners, but are also conscious agents seeking to go beyond their comfort zones and push their abilities into more demanding areas. Arguably, extracurricular activities might attract those with an already greater appetite to push their boundaries.

Overall, these findings confirm the importance to students of live client projects for intra- and entrepreneurial effectiveness (QAA, 2018) and illustrate the perceived value of learning in a transdisciplinary environments (Budwig & Alexander, 2020; Klein et al., 2001; Piaget, 1972). The research also draws out the related perspectives of clients and mentors (see below), which are less often reviewed.

Client Motivations

Three main themes emerged in terms of client motivations: (theme 1) the search for new ideas and fresh eyes; (theme 2) the opportunity to foster University links; and (theme 3) offering students a valuable experience. This reciprocity of perceived benefits is perhaps missing in other accounts of transdisciplinary education, where external partners may come across principally as beneficent providers of student experiences.

Interest in a 'fresh' and 'independent' perspective on their organisations (theme 1) went in tandem with the perceived value of the student cohort in question. This included the potential for multidisciplinary and youthful insights (a combination not easily replicated outside Universities). Client 3, for instance, saw themselves working with the 'coming generation'. While perhaps inexperienced in the world of work, being at this liminal point between education and business practice offered potentially unique approaches to problems and opportunities.

In fostering University links (theme 2), there was an explicit desire to extend business networks in a relatively risk-free engagement. For example, Client 2 talked of 'dipping a toe' in the water, suggesting an openness to the uncertainty involved in the initiative. Client 2 referred to their engagement as an 'experiment', for example, recognising that there were no guaranteed outcomes.

Finally, a recognition of the need for mutual value was evident among the partner businesses (theme 3), with Client 1 citing the desire for 'giving back' – using their own time and resources for the benefit of the students.

Mentor Motivations

Mentors' motivations in taking part in the BCW were more complex than both clients' and students'. These included: (theme 1) an intrinsic interest in working with students on projects; (theme 2) recognition of the value of the initiative to students; (theme 3) the extracurricular nature of the week, in contrast to module teaching; (theme 4) the influence of colleagues and managers; and (theme 5) personal benefits from external engagement. This mix of perspectives is missing in other literature on transdisciplinary education.

On theme 1, Mentor 2 said how they 'liked working on projects with business for students', adding how they enjoy 'the unpredictability of it', as well as – in the case of the BCW – the 'intensity of the week'. Mentor 1 also highlighted a personal interest in experiential learning, which nurtured an alignment of interests. Like the clients, mentors also recognised the value to the students of the BCW (theme 2). As Mentor 1 noted, 'I felt like it's a good opportunity for our students'.

Mentors made explicit contrasts with in-curricular teaching (theme 3), where learning takes place over a longer period and is circumscribed by formalised quality requirements. As Mentor 2 said, 'it was great not to have to do all of the other stuff'. Although, as discussed below, the role of mentor can come with its ambiguities, the attractiveness of the BCW freedoms, compared to modular teaching, also tells us something new about how the extracurricular nature of such initiatives is viewed by academics.

Other colleagues' attitudes affected the mentors' decisions to take part in two distinct ways (theme 4). Firstly, peer endorsement influenced participation. Mentor 3 said, 'I've gotten a very enthusiastic colleague in the room who was taking part'. Secondly, mentors were interested in being helpful to those more senior to them, to get into their 'good books' (Mentor 1). These findings highlight the social and political dynamics at play in recruiting willing members of staff to support such approaches to learning. This political dimension is perhaps missing from previous considerations of the academic role in such learning activities (Beresford & Michels, 2016).

The final theme (theme 5) reveals that mentors' motivations had some affinity with those of the students and the clients. This theme reflected a desire to be 'talking to people out in the real world' (Mentor 1) and staying 'fresh and relevant' (Mentor 2). Unlike the students, though, there was also an anticipation of a more enduring relationship with the client, one that might support research or even a Knowledge Transfer Partnership (Mentor 2). Thus, we can see there is more common ground between academic and business motivations in extracurricular, transdisciplinary education than we might have assumed when looking at it solely from the student's point of view.

EXPERIENCES AND OUTCOMES

The BCW was designed to deliver reciprocal value to students and clients. For the former, the experience and process were central to the outcomes reported.

Student Outcomes

Seven themes were evident from the student data. They covered: (theme 1) benefits from team working; (theme 2) building relationships with clients; (theme 3) being tested and challenged; (theme 4) developing self-confidence; (theme 5) having a story to tell employers; (theme 6) exposure to people from different cultures; and (theme 7) self-understanding and one's place in the world.

Many of the reported outcomes relate directly to the employability benefits associated with this sort of experiential learning (Dalrymple et al., 2021) and the competency framework adopted for this study. A clear majority of students in each case rated as positive how the BCW had enabled them to practise and enhance the four competencies at the heart of the intervention: problem-solving, working with clients, team working and personal competencies (Table 5.1).

Students clearly valued working as a group, which provided benefits over and above boosting capacity (theme 1). As well as offering different ideas in approaching projects, team working also helped students to identify their respective strengths, weaknesses and contributions. Student 1, from outside the Business School, noted how working with the team helped in, 'realising that there is an interface' between business and other aspects of the project they worked on. In other words, an interface existed where the student's relative strengths complemented those of others. Team working also boosted commitments between team members. As this student pointed out, 'nobody wanted to let the others down'. Drawing on the multidisciplinary aspect, Student 2 noted how they'd learned to 'work with different people from different backgrounds' (theme 6).

The experience of working with real-world clients (theme 2) was also important, with Student 1 again noting how they had 'not worked with anybody' in that way before. This was, as they put it, a 'really, really important part of the whole thing'. In this case, the project led to an extended relationship, with the client following up after BCW to offer the student some paid work. In summary, the outcomes reported here in relation to group and client working reveal something about the complex social dynamics involved in such initiatives, something perhaps underplayed in the literature. This goes beyond simply 'breaking out of university solos' (Piaget, 1972) as a format for learning, and shows the rich nature of work in such transdisciplinary settings.

As noted in the discussion of motivations, some students were actively looking for a 'challenge' (theme 3); they were aware of their weaknesses, and where they lacked confidence and experience. In seeking to address this, 'throwing yourself in at the deep end', as Student 1 put it, 'is a really great experience'. Student 2 noted how BCW had also 'challenged me to be a better presenter'. Given that the students also highlighted the help received from clients and mentors in challenging themselves, these sentiments reflect the presence of an environment supportive of student risk-taking.

Having overcome doubts and uncertainties, and delivered outputs the clients found valuable, it is not surprising that some students reported a boost to their self-confidence (theme 4). In reflecting on the BCW, Student 1 said, 'I'm really proud that I did it in the end'. Survey data from the 13 students also show that all respondents felt they'd had the chance to practise and enhance personal resilience skills, a significant majority (9) confirming they'd had this opportunity 'a lot' during the week.

Students were also conscious that the week would boost their standing in job applications and provide practical evidence of their abilities (theme 5). The experience was such that, as Student 1 described it, 'I would now happily attend any kind of interview' given how the BCW 'allowed you to prove yourself'.

The value to students of such learning experiences could be enhanced, however, by greater reflexivity and more attention to lessons acquired beyond the projects themselves. While Budwig and Alexander (2020) see such reflection as a feature of student agency, the current research also highlights the role of mentors in helping students look beyond the problems they are solving for clients. As important as problem-solving is to enterprise education – as highlighted by the QAA (2018), for instance – attention to more enduring learning (such as about client-based working and how to organise time-limited group tasks) should not be lost. There is an additional issue here to do with co-curricular education, which will be discussed later.

Students' self-reporting of being at the threshold of career progression (moving from education to work) highlights how the BCW also provides a liminoid space in which new identities and self-understandings can be sharpened (theme 7). This went beyond greater consciousness of strengths and weaknesses and suggests an increase in perceived self-efficacy. 'I feel like I can do more', as Student 1 described it. Student 2 said that, in the absence of attempting initiatives like the BCW:

[…] you wouldn't even understand yourself … every day is a new day for us (and an opportunity for) understanding who you are. How will you know what you like and what you don't like if you don't challenge your mind?

In this sense, the BCW literally gave students a new story to tell about themselves, not dissimilar to the way that liminoid advertising can help to fashion new consumer identities (Hackley, Hackley, & Bassiouni, 2021).

Overall, the student outcomes suggest that, by engaging with external enterprises and 'real-world' problems, the weeks led to intrapreneurial learning that transcends the university context. This includes working with an external client, generating and screening ideas, planning and managing time-constrained projects, and managing one's contribution as part of a multidisciplinary team. In this sense, as already intimated above, the experience might also contribute to entre-preneurial identity formation (Beresford & Michels, 2016; Gibson & Tavlaridis, 2018), as well as self-perceptions of employability (Ayala Calvo & Manzano García, 2021). The same enrichment of identity and 'value' to others may be true, as will be shown below, for mentors and clients too.

Client Outcomes

The main outcomes for clients were instrumental, including: (theme 1) new ideas and insights; (theme 2) impartial feedback; and (theme 3) adding to the impetus for change.

The first of these links closely to the key motivations clients expressed in get-ting involved in the BCW. Clients accepted that not all outputs could or would be implemented, but they were seen as valuable nonetheless. Client 1 reported that, 'certainly the core messages and tools and ideas that they (the students) came up with are already having a good impact, I would say'.

Client 3 noted the value of the 'completely impartial feedback' the business received (theme 2). In this case, while it didn't provide new thinking as such, it was nonetheless 'helping to confirm that we were doing the right thing'.

Taken together, there is evidence that students' contributions will have long-term consequences. Client 2 said, 'you've given us now the impetus' to look in more detail at requirements for change (theme 3). Client 3 declared that the intervention had been 'quite transformational' and noted that, 'it's also given me another related project'.

These findings highlight how extracurricular, transdisciplinary initiatives can have far-lasting impacts beyond the University and its students. These longer-term and broader outcomes and benefits are missing from some accounts of enterprise education, which remain largely student focused (QAA, 2018).

Mentor Outcomes

Three key outcomes can be discerned here: (theme 1) being part of a mentor com-munity; (theme 2) the positive experience of collaborative problem-solving; and (theme 3) the desire to continue as a mentor.

Theme (1) was reflected in an expressed wish to stay in touch with other men-tors beyond the BCW and wanting the investment of time and relationship-build-ing to have a longer-term pay-off. Mentor 2 said, for instance, 'now we are going back to our day job – and I sort of think that's a shame' as it would be good to 'be able to keep connected in some way'.

Open-ended answers to the survey (from four mentors) revealed themes 2 and 3. Theme 2 centred on the positive experience mentors felt in engaging in collaborative problem-solving with students and clients. Mentor 2 said here:

> Whilst I was initially unsure how this would all play out, I have to say that working with the business partner was one of the highlights for me. It was stimulating and energising to co-create the challenge brief, and the partner's approach of 'seeing what happens' was both reassuring and exactly the attitude needed.

Finally, there was a clear desire (theme 3) to continue as a mentor in future years. Asked about this in the survey, Mentor 1 replied, 'Yes, I will send the organisers an email now to confirm this!'

In this sense, the research reveals the lasting impacts that initiatives like the BCW can have on academic practice and further suggests that enterprise educators widen their interest in the beneficiaries of pedagogical innovation beyond that of the student body.

MUTUAL PERCEPTIONS OF ROLES

As a transdisciplinary and extracurricular activity, the BCW necessarily involved a range of roles, which were both novel and fluid for most if not all participants. Mutual perceptions of – and experience in – these roles – and how to manage and respond to them – were thus a key part of the overall Challenge Week experience and the findings discussed below.

Student Perceptions

The analysis identified seven themes here: (theme 1) the student as a team member; (theme 2) personal strengths and weaknesses; (theme 3) student support and confidence-building; (theme 4) playing to one's strengths; (theme 5) supporting student networking; (theme 6) client being responsive and supportive; and (theme 7) client help with team building.

Given that the initiative was designed around groups of students working on specific client projects, it was unsurprising that team dynamics featured strongly in the findings. In making sense of their own role, students' experiences were not just bound up with both client and mentor interactions, but also their engagements with other students. For the individual, then, there is a strong sense of (theme 1) the student as a team member. There is also reflection on (theme 2) students' personal strengths and weaknesses, given their different programmes of study and personal backgrounds – and a personal evaluation of their potential contribution to the project.

Being part of a group was clearly felt to be positive: all but 1 of the 13 survey respondents confirmed the experience provided a chance 'to practise and enhance team working skills' (8 said 'a lot' and 4 'a little'). But the team-based nature of projects was also a source of frustration and conflict. Student 1 cited the keynote speaker from Day 1 of the week on the need to 'keep it really simple' in addressing projects with significant time constraints. By contrast, the student said they were 'panicking' because their fellow team members were 'going far off track' and 'getting so caught up'.

Perceived strengths and weaknesses were, by implication, relative to other students on the project. As one non-business participant (Student 1) said, 'So working with a team ... I sat there and ... I was focusing on what I didn't know and what ... my weaknesses were'. Students' awareness of themselves as team members thus provided a set of benchmarks through which they perceived their

personal strengths and weaknesses, as well as relative contributions to group performance. While the QAA's (2018) pipeline highlights both students' awareness of
their capabilities and the importance of team working, this research also draws
out the connection between the two.

In addressing this, mentors played a key role in (theme 3) student support
and confidence-building and (theme 4) helping individuals play to their strengths.
Both these points are reflected in the following response from Student 1:

> Well, in my first meeting with my mentor, I said, I can't do this … I have no skills … I was
> really excited with the project, but I thought, I know nothing about all these business (issues).
> So my mentor was really, really perfect and suggested that maybe that was a good thing … in
> that I would be sort of the voice when everybody gets caught up in (the project brief) and I
> could look at it from my own perspective. And as it turns out, that actually is what happened
> in the end.

Mentors also played a role in (theme 5) supporting student networking, mobilis-
ing their networks to put students in touch with relevant people and companies
they might want to talk to.

These examples show how academic mentors can help students engage with
their prior learning and revise their knowledge about the world in the light of
experience (Budwig & Alexander, 2020), with clear benefit in relation to self-
efficacy beliefs as well.

In terms of student perceptions of the clients, out of 13 survey respondents, all
but 2 (who were 'neutral') said their experience was 'positive' (Table 5.1). Student
2 noted how the client 'had time for us' and that 'we were always having meetings'. The student described their team as being 'very, very close'. This also illustrated the key roles of the client in being (theme 6) responsive and supportive and
(theme 7) helping with team building.

Client Perceptions

Client perceptions and experiences fell into seven significant areas: (theme 1) the
search for a mutual exchange of value; (theme 2) a willingness to experiment;
(theme 3) the importance of a good client relationship; (theme 4) clients acting
as mentors; (theme 5) the value of team diversity; (theme 6) the reputation of the
University and its students; and (theme 7) expectations about the academic mentors. These findings have particular resonance as, though the role of the academic
tutor in experiential learning is reasonably well identified in current literature,
that of the client is much less so.

Comments by clients highlighted their perceptions of value in interactions
with students, the University and BCW. As noted previously, clients were particularly keen to generate new ideas on, and insights into, the issues and problems at
the heart of their projects. And while clients were keen to offer students a positive
experience, they also saw this as (theme 1) a mutual exchange of value. Client 1
noted, in contemplating getting involved, that their stance was 'we just need to do
further research to make sure it's a good investment of our time'.

The uncertainty about results also reveals (theme 2) a willingness to experiment. As Client 2 said, 'So this was the first time, so it's a bit of an experiment

to see what we could get out of the project'. The uncertainty about the students involved and the outcomes they'd receive was underlined when the client added, 'we were very lucky; we got a team with one person who was doing a supply chain master's degree ... So we actually had quite a good complementary skill set'.

The importance of a good client relationship (theme 3) was also highlighted here. Client 1 noted how their team 'felt completely comfortable asking for things when they needed them. They knew they'd get a response from us if they did ask'. The role that clients played extended to a perceived scope for (theme 4) clients acting as mentors to students, over and above general support for the project. Client 3 said directly that, 'had I been able to spend more time with the students during the week, then I could have given them more mentoring'.

Clients also recognised the (theme 5) value of team diversity over and above the insights generated, given the student demographic. Client 3 observed how the students, 'came from quite disparate backgrounds in terms of the subjects they were studying, which was a good thing'. This wasn't without consequences, however. As the client noted, some of the students 'didn't know each other' (highlighting an issue that might have been addressed in pre-week preparations). For the project to work, clients recognised it was essential to build an effective relationship with the student team, which even extended to playing a potential mentoring role towards them. So, while clients valued the diversity and capabilities of student teams, the findings also highlight the need for clients to be proactive in making something of this.

Clients' appraisals of students and the project outcomes also revealed the way the BCW shapes (theme 6) the reputation of the University and its students. As Client 1 said, 'These students were a credit to the university. They really were'. For many clients, then, the students' work may be the key lens through which they judge the quality of the University more broadly.

While clients had reasonably clear expectations of the roles that students would play (which appear to have been exceeded in most cases), the same was not always true of the mentor's role (theme 7) – where experiences were not always positive. This was particularly related to perceptions about the degree and nature of mentor input (not all of which would have been seen by the client, of course). Client 1 commented:

> When we started, we were expecting more input from the mentor ... to know that an academic – an expert in the field – was guiding the students. In reality, I don't think the mentor played any part at all, really. But because (the team) were as strong as they were, it wasn't necessary.

Mentor Perceptions

Mentor experience revealed a valuable vein of insights into the BCW dynamics, particularly in terms of their own role and the demands placed upon them. Eight themes were identified here: (theme 1) recognition of the work commitment; (theme 2) freedom from bureaucracy; (theme 3) mentor role ambiguity; (theme 4) the importance of generic mentoring skills; (theme 5) being a team and individual mentor; (theme 6) providing a reality check; (theme 7) helping students reflect on learning; and (theme 8) connecting with real-world practice.

Mentors were not assigned to teams and projects based on 'workload hours', so were taking part voluntarily and 'pro-bono'. Mentors widely requested that the university should in future formally schedule the time commitments. This reflected a broader desire for (theme 1) recognition of the work commitment, with Mentor 1 emphasising that, given the pre-week engagements with the client and team, the 'Challenge Week' was 'probably more like at least a two-week thing'.

One tension in the nature of the role reflected the (theme 2) freedom from bureaucracy but also the (theme 3) mentor role ambiguity. Mentor 2 commented on the 'freedom that this gives', noting 'I really quite like the fact that, because it's extracurricular, there's not a lot of restrictions'. While citing the benefits of a less prescribed role, Mentor 2 also felt this begged the question, 'So what does it mean to be a mentor? Are you meant to teach them anything? (Are you) meant to solve group problems …?'. This suggests the need for further guidance in this area.

Role ambiguity (also, as noted, experienced by the clients at times), and the scope for different mentor behaviours, links to a perceived decentring of disciplinary expertise and the (theme 4) importance of generic mentoring skills. As Mentor 3 said, 'I thought I'd be more required to be more knowledgeable of business management theory than I actually had to be'. Instead, general relationship management, personal coaching and planning skills were needed, including a role in 'firefighting', as Mentor 2 put it.

In exercising these generic skills, BCW mentors also had to balance (theme 5) being a team and an individual mentor. In talking about their students, Mentor 1 said, 'Some of them can do really well. Some of them are totally lost'. Mentor 2 commented that, 'you suddenly find yourself with some student who is so interesting … and who surprises you and really stepped up'. As well as attending to individual needs, the mentor needed to steer the overall team, for example, dealing with some disengaged students (something that potentially reflects the BCW's extracurricular and thus voluntary nature).

Mentors also had a role in (theme 6) providing a reality check. While the BCW gives teams a high degree of autonomy, in order to deliver value to clients, mentors play an important part in appraising students' thinking. Mentor 1 said, 'what I need them to do is take a step back and assess those ideas … Does it fit with the budget (and) … the brief … (and) the capacity resource of the organisation?'

Mentors have a related contribution in (theme 7) helping students reflect on learning. Students tended to focus on the substance of the problem to the neglect of more enduring lessons and transferable skills. Mentor 1 noted the need to get students to ask themselves, 'Have you ever done a project like this before? Have you ever been in a situation where you've had a client like this before?' All this highlights the balancing act required of mentors (and the BCW organising team). The QAA (2018), for instance, notes that, as students move along the enterprise and entrepreneurship pipeline, learning becomes more self-directed. Budwig and Alexander (2020), too, highlight the increase in student agency that should be encouraged.

Mentors also saw their role as a way of (theme 8) connecting with real-world practice – a key incentive for them in taking part in the week. That said, the experience was not always what was expected. Mentor 1, for instance, expressed surprise that the client failed to provide the new insights the mentor was hoping for, noting that the organisation was, 'a bit behind where the academics are with their thinking on these things'.

The tensions detected at times with respect to differing expectations and interpretations about the task and roles at hand – and, for example, about what a mentor or client should be doing – arguably links to the relatively fluid and undirected nature of the extracurricular learning activity of the BCW. It also arguably surfaces examples of the complexities of achieving shared, meaningful language and practice in multiparty, transdisciplinary contexts that characterise such initiatives. These issues will be further considered later in the chapter.

RECOMMENDATIONS FOR FUTURE CHALLENGE WEEKS

The interviewees were specifically asked for advice to those running future BCWs and many survey responses also included such suggestions. Because the seven themes below emerge from all the three participant groups (students, clients and mentors), they are brought together in the following summary.

Chief among the themes was the importance of communication (theme 1). This is critical at all stages of the initiative. Client 1 urged the University to make people more aware of the BCW, adding, 'I think there's a lot of potential for the businesses, but also for the students as well'. For businesses, this might also involve (theme 2) greater clarity on eligibility. As this client also noted, 'our thoughts originally with the Business Challenge were: are we big enough? Are we kind of serious enough to do it?'

The need to orientate the client also emerged (theme 3). Client 2, for instance, talked of the need for 'a broad overview' of the University and its faculties and departments, and where the BCW fitted. This also relates to the importance of (theme 4) managing the client relationship, given that this may endure and develop. Client 1 commented how this was their 'first experience working with students at the University', with Client 2 noting their openness to also work with undergraduate or PhD students.

The importance of communication also extends to (theme 5) transparency on the commitment involved. Mentor 1, for instance, talked about the importance of getting the right 'framing in the mentor's mind'. Student 1 suggested similarly that the organisers should, 'make it more easy to understand', noting that it took them a while to do so. This highlighted a broader issue to do with (theme 6) planning for the week. Both clients and mentors talked about the importance of firming up the project brief and building the team ahead of the main week. Such enhanced 'pre-work' might also facilitate the development of a shared language, the need for which was surfaced earlier, as a means of addressing the complex nature of this sort of transdisciplinary endeavour.

Perhaps inevitably there were reflections on (theme 7) improving the alignment of extracurricular activity with wider programmes of study, including whether the

BCW indeed be should be a week (or longer). On the matter of length, Student 1 said, 'Yeah, one week is fine. Because I'm also looking at the partners, the mentors and the students: (they) will have a lot of things on'. Mentor 2 suggested that the issue might be less to do with whether the week was in-curriculum or not but a matter of timing. When the week takes place outside of teaching semesters, students may have gone home or got a job. As this mentor put it, 'the magic would be if we had (an) extracurricular week, but in term'.

PRACTICE NOTE

This section identifies the lessons learnt for future BCWs, drawing on the research findings and related discussion, as well as on the post-event reflections of the organising team. It also aims to signpost practice issues of wider relevance for readers engaged in similar initiatives.

Communications

Good communication is essential for endeavours that are novel and potentially complex. Participants in the BCWs highlighted the importance of more up-front information in future years. While better scheduling of messaging might be straightforward, other issues related to the challenge of developing a 'shared language'. With the BCW being both transdisciplinary and extracurricular, there is a need to engage audiences from different disciplines in an activity that contains 'business' in the title. One proposal, to improve recruitment of non-business students and mentors, is to work more with trusted, locally embedded advocates (e.g. programme leads, alumni or student representatives across faculties) to explain better what it means for different groups of students.

For clients, communication must respond to the mix of motivations such parties are likely to have. In doing so, messaging will also need to be clear about the commitments involved (both before and during the week itself) in meeting with and supporting mentors and students. One recommendation from the data concerns clarity on eligibility, enabling clients to see whether they should approach the University and what to expect if they do. The importance of helping external parties to understand the University in the round is also evident. This includes explaining internal University structures, and how the BCW fits into teaching, research and outreach. Added to this is the need to manage the client relationship with a view to the longer term. Findings here arguably reinforce the QAA (2018) recommendation of a 'Central Unit' for facilitating enterprise in an institution.

Commitment and Support Requirements

Contrasting behaviours within the student cohort (some were less committed than others, which may reflect the BCW's extracurricular and thus voluntary nature) will always present challenges. Beyond improved pre-week communication clarity, therefore, making the activity 'co-curricular', with the BCW located within an overtly articulated (and rewarded) learning framework, could enhance the attractiveness of the initiative and reduce drop-out rates.

Effective enterprise education requires resources, in this context related to budgets for staff time, as well as facilities and direct costs, such as travel and subsistence. Transparency about the nature of available BCW support – for students, clients and mentors – is vital in securing commitment. As the 2022 data highlighted, many of these issues are inherent in extracurricular activities that rely on academic staff volunteers. If this sort of initiative remains extracurricular and off-timetable, organisers may need to emphasise incentives outside formal workload planning systems. These could include both intrinsic and extrinsic factors. Intrinsic rewards would highlight opportunities for working with clients and students to co-create solutions to real-world problems. Extrinsic factors would foreground links with clients and other mentors that could lead to outputs of value to teaching or research.

In-curricular, Co-curricular or Extracurricular?

As intimated above in discussing student commitment, the organisers continue to discuss whether – and to what extent – the BCW should remain outside the core enterprise-related curriculum. As noted by the mentors, students do not naturally reflect on lessons that transcend problem-solving during the week itself, such as how to work with a client or manage team member contributions. There is potential mileage, therefore, in making such initiatives co-curricular via requirements to engage in a quantified amount of experientially based CPD activity – such as reflective writing linked to the curriculum. Such reflection could capture learning and build a narrative about where the experience fits within students' enterprise and entrepreneurship journeys. Reflection is well understood as an inherently important element of effective enterprise education. A co-curricular framing might thus enable a more explicit mapping of activity along the entrepreneurial learning pipeline.

Cross-faculty Practices

BCW 2021 and 2022 have highlighted challenges in designing enterprise activities that involve students from across faculties. While the BCW clearly responds to an agenda calling for experiences that advance employability and entrepreneurial skills, the literature does not always anticipate the challenges involved in doing this in a transdisciplinary environment. This is more than just a communications issue. For instance, whilst the BCW research shows that the cross-faculty nature of the weeks was attractive to all parties, it required organisers to build a shared vision that worked across multiple boundaries. For example, what makes a project attractive to a Publishing student may be very different from what appeals to a Computing student. To what extent is a shared language possible here? Future practice is likely to require the development of an inclusive proposition, but also one that local advocates can nuance and tailor to appeal to different stakeholders.

Guidance to Mentors

The more facilitative role proposed for the educator in experiential enterprise education is not straightforward to realise, and in the case of the BCW this seemed to cause tensions. Given the importance of mentors to individual student and team performance, any organising team will need to provide clear guidance to mentors on striking a balance between effective team supervision on the one hand and team autonomy on the other. The intention here should be to boost individual and team agency. This may require attention in the pre-week, not least in briefing students on project aims, agreeing suitable methods and deliverables, and clarifying the respective roles of the different BCW participants. Understanding how to support the educator to be a mentor, facilitator and communicator – and even relationship manager with external parties – is a challenge for the organisers and remains a fertile area for future research.

Success Measures

Assessing the success of initiatives like the BCW raises a number of issues. While student reaction and learning are reasonably measurable (such as through post-week questionnaires), changes in behaviour and long-term results for all participants are less easy to track. This remains a work in progress for the BCW research team, but as a minimum a follow-up survey of BCW 'alumni' is one planned new practice. Measuring repeat client and mentor participation and experiences across years can also provide a basis for tracking perceived value beyond the student cohorts.

REFERENCES

Ayala Calvo, J. C., & Manzano García, G. (2021). The influence of psychological capital on graduates' perception of employability: The mediating role of employability skills. *Higher Education Research and Development, 40*(2), 293–308.
Beresford, R., & Michels, N. (2016). To what extent can live projects contribute to creating entrepreneurial learning environments: A critical evaluation of the MBA Enterprise Elective. *Brookes e-learning Journal of Learning and Teaching. 8*(1). ISSN 1744-7747.
Budwig, N., & Alexander, A. J. (2020). A transdisciplinary approach to student learning and development in university settings. *Frontiers of Psychology, 11.* doi:10.3389/fpsyg.2020.576250
Dalrymple, R., Macrae, A., Pal, M., & Shipman, S. (2021). *Employability: A review of the literature 2016–2021.* York: Advance HE.
de Greef, L., Post, G., Vink, C., & Wenting, L. (2017). *Designing interdisciplinary education: A practical handbook for university teachers.* Amsterdam: Amsterdam University Press.
Gaggiotti, H., Jarvis, C., & Richards, J. (2020). The Texture of Entrepreneurship Programs: Revisiting experiential entrepreneurship education through the lens of the liminal–liminoid continuum. *Entrepreneurship Education and Pedagogy, 3*(3), 236–264.
Gibson, D., & Tavlaridis, V. (2018). Work-based learning for enterprise education? The case of Liverpool John Moores University 'live' civic engagement projects for students. *Higher Education, Skills and Work-based Learning, 8*(1), 5–14.
Hackley, C., Hackley, R. A., & Bassiouni, D. H. (2021). Imaginary futures: Liminoid advertising and consumer identity. *Journal of Marketing Communications, 27*(3), 269–283.
Hyams-Ssekasi, D., & Caldwell, E. F. (2018). *Experiential learning for entrepreneurship: Theoretical and practical perspectives on enterprise education.* London: Palgrave Macmillan.
Klein, J. T., Grossenbacher-Mansuy, W., Haberli, R., Bill, A., Scholz, R. W., & Welti, M. (Eds.). (2001). *Transdisciplinarity: Joint problem solving among science, technology, and society.* Basel: Birkhauser Verlag.
Lees, D., Djordjevic, A., & Roberts, R. (2022). Entrepreneurially equipped and employable: A co-curricular approach to developing graduate attributes fit for tackling the wicked problems

faced by our society. In S. Norton & A. Penaluna (Eds.), *3 Es for wicked problems: Employability, enterprise, and entrepreneurship: Solving wicked problems*. York: Advance HE.

Morrissey, J., & Baldry, M. (2022). To be or not to be enterprising? Employability, enterprise, and entrepreneurship solving 'wicked' problems. In S. Norton & A. Penaluna (Eds.), *3 Es for wicked problems: Employability, enterprise, and entrepreneurship: Solving wicked problems*. York: Advance HE.

Norton, S., & Penaluna, A. (Eds.). (2022a). *3 Es for wicked problems: Employability, enterprise, and entrepreneurship: Solving wicked problems*. York: Advance HE.

Norton, S., & Penaluna, A. (2022b). Employability, enterprise, and entrepreneurship: Solving wicked problems: Context and scene setting. In S. Norton & A. Penaluna (Eds.), *3 Es for wicked problems: Employability, enterprise, and entrepreneurship: Solving wicked problems*. York: Advance HE.

Piaget, J. (1972). The epistemology of interdisciplinary relationships. In L. Apostel (Ed.), *Interdisciplinarity: Problems of teaching and research in universities*. Paris: OECD.

Preedy, S., Jones, P., Maas, G., & Duckett, H. (2020). Examining the perceived value of extracurricular enterprise activities in relation to entrepreneurial learning processes. *Journal of Small Business and Enterprise Development, 27*(7), 1085–1105.

QAA. (2018). *Enterprise and entrepreneurship education: Guidance for UK higher education providers*. Gloucester: The Quality Assurance Agency for Higher Education.

Spiegel, A. D. (2011). Categorical difference versus continuum: Rethinking Turner's liminal-liminoid distinction. *Anthropology Southern Africa, 34*(1–2), 11–20.

Turner, V. W. (1974). Liminal to liminoid, in play, flow, and ritual: An essay in comparative symbology. *Rice University Studies, 60*(3), 53–92.

CHAPTER 6

EXTRACURRICULAR ENTERPRISE AND ENTREPRENEURSHIP ACTIVITIES IN HIGHER EDUCATION: UNDERSTANDING ENTREPRENEURIAL COMPETENCIES AND CAPABILITIES

Sarah Preedy[a] and Emily Beaumont[b]

[a]University of Plymouth, Plymouth, UK
[b]University of Gloucestershire, Gloucestershire, UK

ABSTRACT

This chapter examines the role extracurricular activities have in developing higher education (HE) student's entrepreneurial competencies and capabilities. Specifically, this chapter examines: What type of students participate in extracurricular activities? Why do students choose to participate? and What activities offer for entrepreneurial competency and capability development. An electronic survey (e-survey) collected pre- and post-data from two groups: Group A – students participating in extracurricular enterprise and entrepreneurship (EEEx) activities (n = 119); and Group B – students engaged in non-enterprise-related extracurricular activities (n = 72). Findings indicated that students in both groups were motivated to engage in extracurricular activities

Extracurricular Enterprise and Entrepreneurship Activity: A Global and Holistic Perspective
Contemporary Issues in Entrepreneurship Research, Volume 19, 81–95
Copyright © 2024 by Sarah Preedy and Emily Beaumont
Published under exclusive licence by Emerald Publishing Limited
ISSN: 2040-7246/doi:10.1108/S2040-724620240000019006

to enhance their skills, fulfil personal interests and enhance their employability. Utilising Morris, Webb, Fu, and Singhal's (2013) entrepreneurial competencies list as a model, there were found to increase in all but one competency (creativity) for Group A, yet for the control group, most competencies decreased. Independent sample T-tests demonstrated that there was no significant difference in the final ratings of entrepreneurial capability between Group A and Group B, however, the degree of improvement for perceived entrepreneurial capability, pre-to-post, for those participating in enterprise activities was substantially higher than the control group. Finally, students participating in EEEx activities were more likely female, studying a programme within the Business School, and in the second or final stage of their programme. This chapter demonstrates the value that EEEx activities provide in a competency context for students and tasks educators with considering how to develop and signpost specific entrepreneurial competencies and capabilities.

Keywords: Enterprise education; extracurricular; student; competencies; capability; impact

INTRODUCTION

EEEx activities have been recognised as valuable in supplementing in class learning and stimulating student's enterprise knowledge, skills and experience (Neck & Corbett, 2018; Preedy, Jones, Maas, & Duckett, 2020; Watson, McGowan, & Cunningham, 2018). In acknowledgement of the value extracurricular enterprise activities can bring to students, many universities have incorporated them into their wider extracurricular offer, in particular, to focus on the practical component of enterprise and entrepreneurship education (EEEd) (Barnard, Pittz, & Vanevenhoven, 2018; Nabi, Linan, Fayolle, Kreuger, & Walmsley, 2017). This chapter examines HE students' participation in EEEx activities, specifically focusing on what type of students participate in these activities, why they participate and the impact of participation on their entrepreneurial competencies and capability.

Although globally, EEEd is a recognised, and growing, area of the HE curriculum (Bae, Qian, Miao, & Fiet, 2014; Nabi et al., 2017), it faces questioning regarding its utility and impact (Nabi et al., 2017). One common theme in the literature is the difficulty of defining and assessing the necessary traits required of an entrepreneur. More recently, in a move away from focusing solely upon specific 'traits' of entrepreneurial individuals, there has been a focus on EEEd's role in areas such as competency development (Bacigalupo, Kampylis, Punie, & Van den Brande, 2016; Morris et al., 2013). A competency approach to entrepreneurship is not new and has roots in the work of Boyatzis (1982) regarding managerial competencies and Bird's (1995) work on competencies for launching and growing a business. Competencies refer to 'the knowledge, skills, attitudes, values, and behaviours that people need to successfully perform an activity' (Morris et al., 2013, p. 353) and is often built upon structuration theory, which emphasises the reciprocal interactions between individuals and their environments, suggesting that competencies can be enhanced, or conversely decline, over time. Consensus on which competencies are the most 'important' to develop has been difficult to reach (Morris et al., 2013).

The competency approach has been seen as somewhat of an evolution, building upon the solid foundations of research into entrepreneurial traits, knowledge and skills to provide a framework for accelerating entrepreneurial outcomes. Man, Lau, and Chan's (2002) work substantially moved along the direction of competency research by examining how an individual's attributes, skills and knowledge could be combined to categorise and examine their entrepreneurial competencies. Therefore, in the competency approach, the trait perspective is not entirely left behind, traces of a trait perspective can be seen within competencies such as 'risk management' and 'tenacity' (Morris et al., 2013) and 'coping with ambiguity' (Bacigalupo et al., 2016).

One clear advantage of utilising a competency approach is that competencies can be measured against a given standard and therefore improved upon (Bird, 1995). The body of research into entrepreneurial competency, and what benefits competency development brings for entrepreneurial success is becoming established. Competencies are seen to be linked to specific outcomes for individuals, such as increased entrepreneurial intention (Sanchez, 2013), increased entrepreneurial self-efficacy (Liñán & Chen, 2009) and reinforcement of entrepreneurial social capital (Obschonka, Silbereisen, & Schmitt-Rodermund, 2012). Entrepreneurial competency is seen to be important in encouraging successful EEEd outcomes (Čopková, Gróf, Zausinová, & Siničáková, 2023) and in turn EEEd supports the development of entrepreneurial competencies (Hytti, Stenholm, Heinonen, & Seikkula-Leino, 2010; Liñán & Chen, 2009). A better understanding of entrepreneurial competencies can also assist educators in identifying specific educational needs within their cohorts and enhances pedagogical design (Čopková et al., 2023).

The European Commission's Entrepreneurship Competence Framework, EntreComp, identifies 15 competencies over three key areas (Into Action, Ideas and Opportunities and Resources) that encapsulate what it means to be entrepreneurial (Bacigalupo et al., 2016). It originates in earlier calls by the European Commission to increase European citizens entrepreneurial competence; identified as one of the eight competences for lifelong learning (European Parliament and Council, 2006). It has become particularly popular across Europe with its aim to address a lack of common understanding of what specific competencies entrepreneurial activity may involve by offering a comprehensive description of the knowledge, skills and attitudes that people need to be entrepreneurial and create financial, cultural or social value for others. It is intended to be used across sectors and settings and is therefore not restricted to EEEd design and delivery. Such competence frameworks provide a reference point for educators, policymakers and organisations involved in training and education at all levels and these types of frameworks are now prevalent in other areas such as the 'Digital Competence Framework for Citizens' and 'GreenComp' – reference frameworks for digital competence and sustainability competence, both also developed by the European Commission.

Entrepreneurial capability is also an important area of the EEE landscape and goes beyond individual competencies to include the capacity to create, identify and exploit opportunities, as well as to manage and sustain a successful business. Much like the evolution of entrepreneurial behaviour theory, entrepreneurial capability perspectives increasingly recognise that entrepreneurial capabilities can be learned and improved upon. Entrepreneurial capability is often viewed in terms of resources, both external and internal to an individual or firm (Wilson & Martin, 2015). For the purposes of this research, entrepreneurial capability is viewed in terms of individual entrepreneurial capability as opposed to the entrepreneurial capability of firms. Therefore, in an EEEd context, entrepreneurial capability refers to how well a student feels equipped to pursue entrepreneurial opportunities. This involves both external resources and elements, such as prior knowledge, entrepreneurial intention, risk-taking propensity and other socio-cognitive factors (Campo-Ternera, Amar-Sepúlveda, & Olivero-Vega, 2022; Wilson & Martin, 2015). The role that networks, in particular digital networks, play in enhancing an individual's ability to engage in effective entrepreneurial activity is a growing area within the literature (Cenamor, Parida, & Wincent, 2019).

As research into EEEx activities is an emergent area within the wider EEEd research landscape and there is limited understanding of how extracurricular activities impact the formation of entrepreneurial competencies (Arranz, Ubierna, Arroyabe, Perez, & de Arroyabe, 2017), the research was guided by the following questions:

1. What type of students participate in extracurricular activities?
2. Why do students choose to participate in extracurricular activities?
3. What do extracurricular activities offer to students in term of entrepreneurial competencies?
4. What do extracurricular activities offer to students in term of entrepreneurial capability?

METHODOLOGY

This study used an e-survey to gather data from undergraduate students at a post-1992 UK university. The e-survey was administered to two distinct groups: those who participated in EEEx activities (Group A) and those who participated in non-enterprise and entrepreneurship-related extracurricular activities (Group B). A pre- and post-approach was utilised for both groups, however, this differed for each group. Group A completed the online survey pre and post an extracurricular activity, whereas Group B completed the online survey pre and post the academic year to be inclusive of the broad range of extracurricular activities on offer throughout the academic year. Four datasets were therefore collected: Group A pre ($n = 119$); Group A post ($n = 59$); Group B pre ($n = 72$); and Group B post ($n = 31$). This enabled comparisons both within (pre and post) and also between groups.

Both the pre- and post-online surveys contained open and closed questions to provide quantitative and qualitative data regarding; participants' motivations for engaging in the activity, their perceptions of entrepreneurial competency gains (or not), and perceptions of their own entrepreneurial capabilities. Each student was given a unique identifying number that enabled researchers to track students while ensuring anonymity.

A list of entrepreneurial competencies validated in the work of Morris et al. (2013) was utilised as a framework in this study. This list of competencies was generated via a three-round Delphi study which is a highly formalised method of soliciting ideas and subsequently gaining consensus among individuals considered to be experts in the field of interest. The Delphi panel included 20 distinguished entrepreneurs, representing a range of industries, and 20 Professors of entrepreneurship with at least 10 years of EEEd experience and research outputs. The 13 entrepreneurial competencies that were agreed upon by the panel were tested with a sample of HE students (pre- and post-testing) who were all involved in 6-week intensive enterprise programme that provided consulting support to entrepreneurs with struggling businesses.

The types of extracurricular activities offered at the UK university sampled in this study differed markedly from those undertaken by participants in the Morris et al. (2013) study that specifically focused on enterprise and entrepreneurship activities. Therefore, the list of competencies was adapted accordingly to suit a more general list of activities being undertaken beyond enterprise and entrepreneurship. This included the removal of 'resource leveraging' and 'value creation' due to their strong association with venture creation. The final list utilised in this study was as follows (and in no particular priority order); effectual reasoning, networking, leadership, creativity, self-efficacy, interpersonal skills, resilience, locus of control, tolerance of ambiguity, alertness to opportunities, opportunity exploitation, increased confidence, perseverance and risk-taking. There is also considerable overlap between this list of 14 competencies and the 15 competencies utilised in the Entrecomp framework demonstrating alignment between this study and other research in the entrepreneurial competency area.

Participants were given a description of each competency to aid them in their understanding, for example, language such as 'self-efficacy' is not necessarily commonly used by the student population, and so an explanation from the literature was provided. Participants would list what entrepreneurial competencies they expected to gain prior to engaging with an extracurricular activity and then after engagement list what competencies they feel they actually did gain thereby measuring, from their perspective, whether the intervention (the extracurricular activity) had resulted in the gaining of specific competencies.

To measure entrepreneurial capability, participants were given a definition of entrepreneurial capability 'defined as an ability to recognise and exploit opportunities' and a scale of 1–10 (1 = No ability to be entrepreneurially capable; 10 = Fully able to be entrepreneurially capable) to self-rate their entrepreneurial capability at that point in time. All participants completed this rating before engagement in an extracurricular activity and then again afterwards thereby measuring

whether the intervention (the extracurricular activity) had resulted in a positive
or negative perception of their entrepreneurial capability.

Following data collection, survey data was analysed qualitatively and quan-
titatively with the assistance of appropriate analysis tools (NVIVO and SPSS).
Descriptive statistics were utilised to ascertain the types of students who engaged
with extracurricular activities and to measure pre- and post-scores for competencies and capabilities. Comparisons were made between Group A and Group B to
ascertain the impact engagement in EEEx activities had upon perceived entrepreneurial competency and capability development.

Thematic analysis of the open-text responses enabled a greater understanding
of the motivations of the students for engagement with extracurricular activity.

FINDINGS AND DISCUSSION

What Type of Students Participate in Extracurricular Activities?

To provide context on the types of extracurricular activities available at the sampled university. Typical activities participated in by Group A included; hack-
a-thons, pitch practice and delivery sessions, speed networking, business plan
competitions and guest speaker events. Group B activities included in order of
popularity; music, arts or popular culture (i.e. DJ society and Viking Society),
Sports (i.e. Kayaking and Archery), volunteering or charity (i.e. Amnesty
International) or study-related activities (i.e. Marine Biology club).

Female respondents outnumbered male respondents for both Group A and
Group B (see Table 6.1). As around 56% of the total student body at the sampled
university was female at the time of data collection, these figures are roughly
representative of the wider population. However, there was a slightly higher proportion of female students engaging in enterprise and entrepreneurship-specific
extracurricular activities than non-enterprise and entrepreneurship. This challenges the literature which suggests that males often have greater entrepreneurial
intention levels than females (Bae et al., 2014) and that women can face barriers
to engaging with EEEd, due to lower self-efficacy and confidence rates, but also
due to a prevalence of masculine discourse in relation to EEEd activity (Jones &
Warhaus, 2018; Westhead & Solesvik, 2016).

In terms of ethnicity, Group A had a more diverse group of students. In 2016,
the year of data collection, figures for the sampled university show that around
83% of the total student body was White (British or Other), and this proportion

Table 6.1. Gender split of sample.

Group	Male	Female	Unknown/Other
Group B (Pre)	27 (37.5%)	44 (61.1%)	1 (1.4%)
Group B (Post)	14 (45.2%)	16 (51.6%)	1 (3.2%)
Group A (Pre)	48 (40.3%)	70 (58.8%)	1 (0.8%)
Group A (Post)	18 (30.5%)	32 (54.2%)	9 (15.3%)

is reflected in Group B but not in Group A where 78% of respondents identified as White British, with the second-largest category being Asian or Asian-British Chinese attendees and only the third largest being 'Other White'. This suggests that EEEx activities were slightly more inclusive to Black, Asian and minority ethnic (BAME) students.

In terms of student discipline area, the majority of Group A respondents (67%) were studying programmes within the Business School. This situation is not unusual, as several studies have identified the concentration of enterprise and entrepreneurship activities both in curricular and extracurricular, within business schools (Preedy et al., 2020; Turner & Gianiodis, 2018). Students within a Business School are more likely to be exposed to EEEd in their curriculum than in other schools, there it is likely that these students may be more likely to take an interest in EEEx activities. However, it must be acknowledged that marketing and advertising of these activities may be primarily to Business School students (Preedy & Jones, 2015).

Students who participated in extracurricular enterprise activities were also more likely to be in the second (40%) or final/third year of their studies (34%). This may be due to students closer to graduation being more pre-occupied about their next steps including their employability prospects (Gedye & Beaumont, 2020; Nabi, Walmsley, Liñán, Akhtar, & Neame, 2018).

Why Do Students Choose to Participate in Extracurricular Activities?

Group A was asked in the pre-survey about their motivations to engage. Table 6.2 summarises the key themes that emerged. Where answers cited multiple factors, the most prominent reason was coded (e.g. 'fun, engaging and great network opportunity' was judged to fit best under category 4, as two factors of enjoyment or socialising were mentioned vs. one factor of generally positive experiences).

Table 6.2 demonstrates the importance of skills development for many participants. Their engagement in extracurricular activity was closely linked to a desire to improve their interpersonal skills – the most common reason given for attendance was related to generalised life skills or self-development – motivation, inspiration, knowledge and understanding – and not specific business skills. Considering the emphasis across universities worldwide on 'soft' skills development (Cimatti, 2016) this shows a strategic focus for participants as opposed to extracurricular activities purely being for fun or socialising which might be the more traditional perspective of their function. Expectations were also consistently positive, students were optimistic about learning something new, even when they did not have a specific idea of what this might be.

These results also show that respondents consistently had career-focused expectations, seeing enterprise and entrepreneurship activities as a route to enhancing their employability. Perhaps this also indicates high expectations of extracurricular activities, not only do they serve those considering entrepreneurship as their next step but also more generally assist students with their employability prospects regardless of discipline area, educational attainment or level of study.

Table 6.2.   Motivation to engage in enterprise extracurricular activities ($n = 110$).

Category	Description	Number of Respondents	Examples
1	An expectation related to generalized skills or positive experiences	47	'knowledge', 'positive way of thinking', 'self-development'
2	Sustainability, social enterprise or community-focussed expectation	26	'gain information around enterprise/community projects', 'to better my understanding of sustainable business', 'a better understanding of social enterprises'
3	An aim of gaining career or business skills	24	'to gain insight on how to do better presentations', 'develop insight to business world and life as an entrepreneur'
4	An expectation of primarily enjoyment networking or socializing	9	'fun', 'it would be funny'
5	No defined aim, or a negative expectation	4	'hopefully a pleasant surprise', 'open-minded- I'll find out'

There is recognition in the literature of an overlap between the skills, attributes and competencies of employability, and enterprise and entrepreneurship (Decker-Lange, 2021; QAA, 2018). Norton (2019) describes this as a 'blurring' with components of enterprise fundamental to the components of employability and *vice versa*. Walmsley, Decker-Lange, and Lange (2022) noted 'substantial overlap' in the skills that are deemed critical to both entrepreneurship and employability with Decker-Lange (2021) describing enterprise, entrepreneurship and employability as the '3E's, which are closely related concepts within the HE sector (Beaumont, 2023).

The motivations of Group B were also assessed in the survey ($n = 72$), the most common, in order of frequency, were:

1. Socialising, networking (e.g. 'a wider social network of friends', 'building more networks', 'friends/wider social life' and 'spending time with like-minded people').
2. Enjoyment and life skills (e.g. 'fun', 'personal development', 'laughs' and 'discipline').
3. Health (e.g. 'increased fitness', 'healthy life' and 'relieve stress and keep fit and healthy').
4. Career and business skills (e.g. 'get some idea about opportunities after studies', 'additions to my CV and further experience and skills' and 'qualifications in certificate form').
5. Studies (e.g. 'Network to gain further knowledge. Also like-minded people who may help with my own degree').
6. Other (e.g. a spiritual or niche interest benefit, such as becoming more involved in a religion or improving at skiing).

Despite the simplicity that Table 6.2 and the above list imply, for both Groups A and B, differing motivations were often intertwined. Participants utilised the open-text response boxes to discuss multiple motivations in tandem seeing links between the social and professional parts of their development. However, for Group B, there appeared to be a stronger focus on socialising, generalised life skills or physical fitness. Surprisingly, in both groups, improving study skills or gaining university-related benefits was barely mentioned, suggesting participants did not see extracurricular activities as a platform for these academic gains. The clearest commonality between the two groups can be seen regarding an employability focus with Group B more explicit in this motivation including statements about enhancing their CV through extracurricular activity engagement or identifying specific activities that may assist them towards industry/professional level certification.

What Do Extracurricular Activities Offer to Students in Terms of Entrepreneurial Competencies?

Students in all four datasets were asked to identify which out of the competencies based on the list modelled on Morris et al. (2013), they expected to gain (which provided a rationale for engagement or competency gap coverage). Upon completion, they were asked what competencies they perceived they had actually gained. An additional option of 'Other' was provided for participants who felt the competency list provided was not exhaustive and to help identify the value added from extracurricular activities. However, responses for this were few and have been discounted as answers were around cognitive development rather than competencies. Figs. 6.1–6.3 illustrate the percentage of total respondents (Group A and Group B) who rated themselves as expecting to possess (pre) and then possessing (post) a particular competency.

For some of the competencies, there were particularly high starting expectations for both groups (i.e. Networking) and for other competencies much lower starting expectations (i.e. Locus of control). There were marked differences in starting expectations between Group A and Group B for specific competencies. For 'Resilience', only 7.1% of Group A thought this competency would be developed compared with 43.8% of Group B. For 'Increased Confidence', only 32.1%

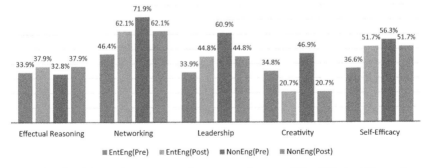

Fig. 6.1. Participants' competency increase or decrease (%) – Effectual Reasoning, Networking, Leadership, Creativity and Self-Efficacy.

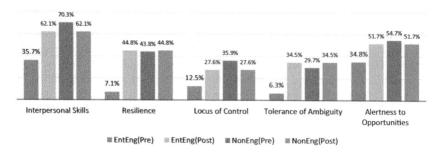

Fig. 6.2. Participants' competency increase or decrease (%) – Interpersonal Skills, Resilience, Locus of Control, Tolerance of Ambiguity and Alertness to Opportunities.

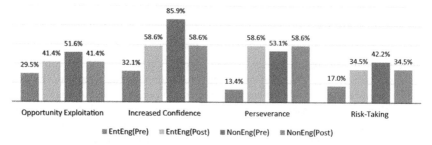

Fig. 6.3. Participants' competency increase or decrease (%) – Opportunity Exploitation, Increased confidence, Perseverance, Risk-taking.

of Group A thought this would be developed compared with 85.9% of Group B. Overall, Group A was more cautious in what they expected to develop.

For all competencies, bar 'creativity', Group A perceived an improvement in their entrepreneurial competencies. However, for Group B, 10 of the 15 competencies decreased, with several rather dramatically, while only 5 increased, and these only slightly. The slighter increases seen in Group B was perhaps unsurprising considering the initial higher expectations.

For Group A, particularly large gains were seen in the entrepreneurial competencies of Resilience (7.1–44.8%) and Perseverance (13.4–58.6%). The only category where a decrease was seen over time was Creativity (34.8–20.7%). These findings suggest that EEEx activities are more appropriate platform for entrepreneurial competency development than non-EEEx activities, although it is possible for some entrepreneurial competencies to be developed through engagement in non-EEEx activity.

What Do Extracurricular Activities Offer to Students in Terms of Entrepreneurial Capability?

All participants were asked to rate their perceived entrepreneurial capability prior to engagement in extracurricular activity and again afterwards. The scale was 0–10 with 0 indicating the lowest level of entrepreneurial capability and 10 the highest.

For Group B, the mean rating was 7.01 in the pre-survey ($n = 72$) with a con-centration of responses in the ratings of 5, 6 and 7. Considering none of the participants were studying EEEd, nor were engaged in any EEEx activities, this was a particularly positive initial self-perception of their entrepreneurial capabil-ity. In the post-survey ($n = 31$), the mean had shifted slightly higher to 7.8 with responses concentrated in the ratings of 7 and 8. There was also an elimination of the extremely lower ratings in the results, none of the post-survey participants rated themselves 1 or 2 further indicating an increased positive self-perception of entrepreneurial capability as a result of engaging in extracurricular activity.

By comparison, the mean rating by Group A in the pre-survey results ($n = 117$) was lower, 6.55 compared to 7.01. Ratings were concentrated around the numbers 5 and 6 with a higher proportion, than Group B, rating themselves in the lowest categories, and very few rating themselves in the highest catego-ries. This follows the pattern of the earlier competency results where Group A appeared to be more cautious in their ratings than Group B. The mean improved for Group As between pre- and post-survey, from 6.55 to 7.36 indicating that perception of their entrepreneurial capabilities was improved by attending EEEx activities. However, Group B still rated themselves slightly higher (7.87 vs. 7.36).

Independent sample T-test showed that there was no significant difference in the final ratings between Groups A and B ($P = 0.240$, 2-tailed, $df = 73$). The difference in ratings between these two groups before they attended any extracur-ricular events was even less significant ($P = 0.115$, 2-tailed, $df = 187$). There were, however, significant differences between the pre- and post-outcomes within each group: Group B ($P = 0.047$, 2-tailed, $df = 64$) and Group A ($P = 0.013$, 2-tailed, $df = 159$).

Thus, although Group A still ended with a slightly lower score when reflecting on their entrepreneurial capabilities, their degree of improvement across capabili-ties was significantly higher. This is a key point to note, as it means EEEx activi-ties increased participants' rating from baseline more than other extracurricular activities, even if they did not produce a significantly higher final rating.

CONCLUSION

In conclusion, this study has shown that students engaged in EEEx activities are more likely to be female, from a BAME group, studying a programme within the Business School and in the second or final stage of their programme. Those engaged in EEEx activities tended to have a soft skills and employability focus and expectation of the extracurricular activities they engaged in. In comparison, the motivations of those not engaged in enterprise and entrepreneurship activities were often more related to socialising, generalised life skills or physical fitness but showed commonality in a focus on employability also.

Group A saw improvements from pre to post in their rating of all competencies, bar 'creativity'. Whereas Group B saw a decrease in 10 of the 15 competencies, several rather dramatically highlighting the significance in improving entrepreneur-ial competencies through engagement in EEEx activities. Finally, the mean rating of entrepreneurial capability improved between Group A pre- and post-results. However, Group B participants still rated themselves more highly (7.87 vs. 7.36). However, Group A started at a lower self-perceived rating of entrepreneurial capability and increased much more. Given that several of Group B rated themselves very highly in both cases, this may point to a more realistic view, before and after, among students drawn to enterprise and entrepreneurship activities, as well as a greater overall impact of the events. After all, if they are engaged in enterprise and entrepreneurship activities, they perhaps have a better understanding of entrepreneurial capability, leading to a more realistic, albeit lower, rating.

There are implications for practice regarding the type of student extracurricular activities may attract and the benefits that participants draw from participation. Within this study, EEEx activities attracted a large proportion of students from business disciplines. This has implications for EEEd in considering whether they market to and deliver EEE to students from a diverse range of discipline areas. Great strides have been made in this area in recent years with an increased focus on interdisciplinary approaches to EEEd within universities. However, the extent to which the advances within interdisciplinary EEE curricula activity have translated to the extracurricular arena is debated (Preedy et al., 2020).

Regarding competencies, offering a framework for students to understand what the gains are from participation in EEEd appears to be beneficial. It is also a useful evaluative tool for educators and universities to understand better the impact that both EEEx and non- EEEx activities have for participants. Considering the threat these activities face in terms of funding and resources (Preedy & Jones, 2015), being able to demonstrate measurable impact such as competency development offers an evidence-based tool for justifying such activities existence. One cautionary note in these findings could be the students' own recognition of competencies. Volumes of education theory articles have been written on the difficulties students experience in recognising their own skills and in applying them in differing contexts – and this is known to impact on students' understanding of concepts like 'graduate attributes' and 'employability' too. Likewise, experts in a field – entrepreneurship included – are known to perceive the skills and knowledge of their field differently to a novice. Therefore, EEEds may also benefit from a greater understanding and more targeted signposting of the competencies that can be developed through extracurricular activities to alleviate such difficulties.

FURTHER RESEARCH

There are several further areas to explore in this developing research area. Previous literature and this study focus on single institutions and therefore, going forward, a multi-institutional study, allowing comparisons across the HE sector, would be advantageous. A qualitative methodology would also allow for a deeper exploration of students' perceptions and understandings of their competencies. The inclusion of interviews with EEEds would also provide a comparison between intended delivery (by educators) and perceived impact (on the students). This study was completed prior to the widespread uptake of Entrecomp which has since become a key competency framework for EEEd across Europe. Although the competencies chosen to examine in this study overlap with the competencies listed in Entrecomp, further research examining the impact of extracurricular activities utilising Entrecomp as the specified framework for measurement would be of interest.

PRACTICE NOTE

We hope that the findings discussed in this chapter can act as an inspiration for educators (both EEEx and non-EEEx) in the design of their pedagogical activities and provide guidance for students in enhancing their educational journey. Below are some suggested recommendations for educators and students.

Recommendations for Educators

• Offering a framework for students to understand what the gains are from participation in extracurricular activities, both enterprise and non-enterprise focused. There are numerous competency frameworks available, with some chosen frameworks outlined in the full chapter, but educators must choose those that are most relevant to their own educational contexts.
• Widening the marketing and dissemination of EEEx activities to ensure reach to students outside of the Business School. This can aid the inclusivity of activities and encourage multidisciplinary approaches.

Recommendations for Students

• To consider participation in extracurricular activities earlier in the educational journey. Engagement in extracurriculars can advance knowledge, skills and experience, and early participation will allow an extended period for building on such strengths.
• To consider existing competencies and potential competency gain during time spent at university. Graduate employers are increasingly recruiting individuals based upon the demonstration of many of the entrepreneurial competencies discussed in this chapter. The 3E's are intertwined and engagement in EEEx activities may subsequently advance graduate employability prospects alongside entrepreneurial ambitions.

REFERENCES

Arranz, N., Ubierna, F., Arroyabe, M. F., Perez, C., & de Arroyabe, J. C. F. (2017). The effect of curricular and extracurricular activities on university students' entrepreneurial intention and competences. *Studies in Higher Education*, *42*(11), 1979–2008. doi:10.1080/03075079.2015.1130030

Bacigalupo, M., Kampylis, P., Punie, Y., & Van den Brande, G. (2016). *EntreComp: The entrepreneurship competence framework*. Luxembourg: Publication Office of the European Union.

Bae, T. J., Qian, S., Miao, C., & Fiet, J. O. (2014). The relationship between entrepreneurship education and entrepreneurial intentions: A meta-analytic review. *Entrepreneurship Theory and Practice*, *38*(2), 217–254.

Barnard, A., Pittz, T., & Vanevenhoven, J. (2018). Entrepreneurship education in U.S. community colleges: A review and analysis. *Journal of Small Business and Enterprise Development*, *26*(2), 90–208.

Beaumont, E. (2023). One for all and all for one: The 3Es (employability, enterprise and entrepreneurship). In S. Hansen & K. Daniels (Eds.), *How to enable the employability of university graduates* (pp. 179–187). https://doi.org/10.4337/9781803926513.00034. eISBN: 9781803926513.

Bird, B. (1995). Toward a theory of entrepreneurial competency. In J. Katz (Ed.), *Advances in entrepreneurship firm emergence & growth* (pp. 52–72). Greenwich, CT: JAI Press.

Boyatzis, R. (1982). *The Competent Manager – A model for effective performance*. New York, NY: John Wiley & Sons.

Campo-Ternera, L., Amar-Sepúlveda, P., & Olivero-Vega E. (2022). Interaction of potential and effective entrepreneurial capabilities in adolescents: Modeling youth entrepreneurship structure using structural equation modelling. *Journal of Innovation and Entrepreneurship*, *11*(1). https://doi.org/10.1186/s13731-022-00201-y

Cenamor, J., Parida, V., & Wincent, J. (2019). How entrepreneurial SMEs compete through digital platforms: The roles of digital platform capability, network capability and ambidexterity. *Journal of Business Research*, *100*, 196–206.

Cimatti, B. (2016). Definition, development, assessment of soft skills and their role for the quality of organizations and enterprises. *International Journal for Quality Research*, *10*(1), 97–130.

Čopková, R., Gróf, M., Zausinová, J., & Siničáková, M. (2023). Adaptation of the Entrepreneurship Competences Questionnaire: When entrepreneurship is more than just business. *Strategic Management*, 46. doi:10.5937/straman2300046c

Decker-Lange, C. (2021). Three reasons why we should think about employability in entrepreneurship education. Centre for Innovation in Legal and Business Education (SCiLAB). http://www.open.ac.uk/blogs/scilab/index.php/2021/03/08/three-reasons-why-we-should-think-about-employability-in-entrepreneurship-education/

Decker-Lange, C., Lange, K., Dhaliwal, S., & Walmsley, A. (2022). Exploring entrepreneurship education effectiveness at British universities – An application of the World Café method. *Entrepreneurship Education and Pedagogy*, *5*(1), 113–136. https://doi.org/10.1177/2515127420935391

European Parliament and Council. (2006). Recommendation of the European Parliament and of the Council of 18 December 2006 on key competences for lifelong learning. *Official Journal of the European Union*. Retrieved from https://eur-lex.europa.eu/LexUriServ/LexUriServ.do?uri=OJ:L:2006:394:0010:0018:en:PDF

Gedye, S., & Beaumont, E. (2020). The ability to get a job: Student understandings and definitions of employability. *Education + Training*, *60*(5), 406–420. doi:10.1108/ET-10-2017-0159

Hytti, U., Stenholm, P., Heinonen, J., & Seikkula-Leino, J. (2010). Perceived learning outcomes in entrepreneurship education: The impact of student motivation and team behaviour. *Education + Training*, *52*(8/9), 587–606. https://doi.org/10.1108/00400911011088935

Jones, S., & Warhaus, J. P. (2018). This class is not for you. *Journal of Small Business and Enterprise Development*, *25*(2), 182–200.

Liñán, F., & Chen, Y. (2009). Development and cross–cultural application of a specific instrument to measure entrepreneurial intentions. *Entrepreneurship Theory and Practice*, *33*(3), 593–617. https://doi.org/10.1111/j.1540-6520.2009.00318.x

Man, T. W., Lau, T., & Chan, K. F. (2002). The competitiveness of small and medium enterprises: A conceptualization with focus on entrepreneurial competencies. *Journal of Business Venturing*, *17*, 123–142. https://doi.org/10.1016/S0883-9026(00)00058-6

Morris, M. H., Webb, J., Fu, J., & Singhal, S. (2013). A competency-based perspective on entrepreneurship education: Conceptual and empirical insights. *Journal of Small Business Management*, *51*(3), 352–369.

Nabi, G., Linan, F., Fayolle, A., Kreuger, N., & Walmsley, A. (2017). The impact of entrepreneurship education in higher education. *Academy of Management Learning and Education*, *16*(2), 1–23.

Nabi, G., Walmsley, A., Liñán, F., Akhtar, I., & Neame, C. (2018). Does entrepreneurship education in the first year of higher education develop entrepreneurial intentions? The role of learning and inspiration. *Studies in Higher Education, 43*(3), 452–467. doi:10.1080/03075079.2016.1177716

Neck, H. M., & Corbett, A. C. (2018). The scholarship of teaching and learning entrepreneurship. *Entrepreneurship Education and Pedagogy, 1*(1), 8–41.

Norton, S. (2019). Enterprise: An approach to enhancing employability. Retrieved from https://www.advance-he.ac.uk/news-and-views/enterprise-approach-enhancing-employability

Obschonka, M., Silbereisen, R. K., & Schmitt-Rodermund, E. (2012). Explaining entrepreneurial behavior: Dispositional personality traits, growth of personal entrepreneurial resources, and business idea generation. *The Career Development Quarterly, 60*(2), 178–190. https://doi.org/10.1002/j.2161-0045.2012.00015.x

Preedy, S., & Jones, P. (2015). An investigation into university extra-curricular enterprise support provision. *Education + Training, 57*(8/9), 992–1008.

Preedy, S., Jones, P., Maas, G., & Duckett, H. (2020). Examining the benefits of extracurricular enterprise activities in relation to entrepreneurial learning processes. *Journal of Small Business and Enterprise Development, 27*(7), 1085–1105.

QAA. (2018). *Enterprise and entrepreneurship education: Guidance for UK higher education.* York: Quality Assurance Agency.

Sanchez, J. C. (2013). The impact of an entrepreneurship education program on entrepreneurial competencies and intention. *Journal of Small Business Management, 51*(3), 447–465.

Turner, T., & Gianiodis, P. (2018). Entrepreneurship unleashed: Understanding entrepreneurial education outside of the Business School. *Journal of Small Business Management, 56*(1), 131–149. doi:10.1111/jsbm.12365

Walmsley, A., Decker-Lange, C., & Lange, K. (2022). Conceptualising the entrepreneurship education and employability nexus. In G. J. Larios-Hernandez, A. Walmsley, & I. Lopez-Castro (Eds.), *Theorising undergraduate entrepreneurship education: Reflections on the development of the entrepreneurship education* (pp. 97–114). Cham: Palgrave Macmillan.

Watson, K., McGowan, P., & Cunningham, J. A. (2018). An exploration of the Business Plan Competition as a methodology for effective nascent entrepreneurial learning. *International Journal of Entrepreneurial Behavior & Research, 24*(1), 121–146.

Westhead, P., & Solesvik, M. Z. (2016). Entrepreneurship education and entrepreneurial intention: Do female students benefit? *International Small Business Journal, 34*(8), 979–1003. https://doi-org.plymouth.idm.oclc.org/10.1177/0266242615612534

Wilson, N., & Martin, L. (2015). Entrepreneurial opportunities for all? Entrepreneurial capability and the capabilities approach. *The International Journal of Entrepreneurship and Innovation, 16*(3), 159–169.

INDEX

Printed and bound by CPI Group (UK) Ltd, Croydon, CR0 4YY

15/04/2024

14483920-0003